Lear's Labour's Lost

A new play by William Shakespeare & Jeff Goode

Single copies of plays are sold for reading purposes only. The copying or duplicating of a play, or any part of play, by hand or by any other process, is an infringement of the copyright. Such infringement will be vigorously prosecuted.

Baker's Plays
7611 Sunset Blvd.
Los Angeles, CA 90042
bakersplays.com

NOTICE

This book is offered for sale at the price quoted only on the understanding that, if any additional copies of the whole or any part are necessary for its production, such additional copies will be purchased. The attention of all purchasers is directed to the following: this work is fully protected under the copyright laws of the United States of America, the British Commonwealth, including Canada, and all other countries of the Copyright Union. Violations of the Copyright Law are punishable by fine or imprisonment, or both. The copying or duplication of this work or any part of this work, by hand or by any process, is an infringement of the copyright and will be vigorously prosecuted.

This play may not be produced by amateurs or professionals for public or private performance without first submitting application for performing rights. Royalties are due on all performances whether for charity or gain, or whether admission is charged or not. Since performance of this play without the payment of the royalty fee renders anybody participating liable to severe penalties imposed by the law, anybody acting in this play should be sure, before doing so, that the royalty fee has been paid. Professional rights, reading rights, radio broadcasting, television and all mechanical rights, etc. are strictly reserved. Application for performing rights should be made directly to BAKER'S PLAYS.

No one shall commit or authorize any act or omission by which the copyright of, or the right to copyright, this play may be impaired. No one shall make any changes in this play for the purpose of production.

Publication of this play does not imply availability for performance. Both amateurs and professionals considering a production are strongly advised in their own interest to apply to Baker's Plays for written permission before starting rehearsals, advertising, or booking a theatre.

Whenever the play is produced, the author's name must be carried in all publicity, advertising and programs. Also, the following notice must appear on all printed programs, "Produced by special arrangement with Baker's Plays."

Licensing fees for *LEAR'S LABOUR'S LOST* is based on a per performance rate and payable one week in advance of the production.

Please consult the Baker's Plays website at www.bakersplays.com or our current print catalogue for up to date licensing fee information.

Copyright © 2009 by Jeff Goode
Made in U.S.A.
All rights reserved.

LEAR'S LABOUR'S LOST
ISBN 978-0-87440-190-5
#1845-B

GENERAL PREFACE TO THE SERIES

They say that familiarity breeds contempt and there is no playwright, living or dead, whose work is more familiar to audiences the world over, than William Shakespeare. Four hundred years of almost continuous production, adaptation and recitation have ensured that even the completely uninitiated have a working knowledge of the Bard that can render some of his finest works formulaic.

What grade-schooler doesn't know that the love affair in ROMEO AND JULIET turns out badly? Or that the famous speech in HAMLET goes: "To be, or not to be, yadda yadda yadda…"? And in a medium where suspense is everything—where dramatic twists and comic turns both depend upon the element of surprise—having such a well-versed fan-base can be problematic. Ironically, the most gifted dramatist in history is often hard-pressed to impress our jaded modern audience, simply because it is impossible to remove their foreknowledge of the story and allow them to experience the plays in the unadulterated context in which Shakespeare's contemporaries saw them for the very first time.

The New Plays of William Shakespeare were developed as a means to a fresh perspective on these classic texts. Each play in the series intertwines two of the extant works to create an original script with authentically Shakespearean language, verse and characters, in new and unexpected situations whose outcome may still be in doubt.

The plays in this series are designed to be read, performed and enjoyed just as you would the traditional works of Shakespeare. Performers familiar with the canon will find that great lengths have been taken to preserve the integrity and intention of the original verse, rhyme and imagery. Conventions of Elizabethan stagecraft, dramaturgical analysis and scansion apply to the new plays as to the originals. Only the action is up in the air.

The series also seeks to address challenges common to present day production companies, such as cast size and imbalance of male and female roles.

It is hoped that these plays might offer both performers and audiences new insight into the genius and mastery of Shakespeare, freed of a few centuries' preconception, and perhaps with a few surprises still intact.

LEAR'S LABOUR'S LOST was first performed May 4th, 2008, at the Attic Theatre Center in Los Angeles.

Producing Artistic Director: James Carey
Artistic Director: Brian Shnipper

KING LEAR .... William Salyers
COSTARD ....Mark Fite
KENT.. Eric Jorgenson
GLOUCESTER.................................. David Fruechting
EDMUND.................................... Eric Curtis Johnson
EDGAR ....David Paul Wichert

PRINCESS ....Johanna McKay
GONERIL .... Robin Roy
REGAN ....Tisha Terrasini Banker
CORDELIA ....Kathleen Rose Perkins
JAQUENETTA............................... Nora L. Frankovich
BOYET... Allynde Joseph

OSWALD .... Dane Whitlock
NARRATION .... Adam Hahn

LEAR'S NAVARRE

Setting aside his sword, after a lifetime of battle, retiring King Lear doffs his crown and sues for peace to the rival French, hoping to leave his kingdom in the care of his three beloved daughters, and dedicate himself and his court to philosophical pursuits.

The king's loyal confidantes, the earls of Kent and Gloucester, as well as Costard the fool, have agreed to join him in three years of scholarly contemplation, enforced by vows of abstinence and strict royal edicts to that effect.

DRAMATIS PERSONAE

LEAR, *King of Navarre*
EARL OF KENT
EARL OF GLOUCESTER
COSTARD, *Lear's fool*
EDGAR, *Gloucester's elder son*
EDMUND, *Gloucester's younger, bastard son*

PRINCESS, *daughter of the King of France*
BOYET, *a lady attending the Princess*
GONERIL, *Lear's eldest daughter*
REGAN, *Lear's second daughter*
CORDELIA, *Lear's youngest daughter*
JAQUENETTA, *a maidservant*

OSWALD, *a steward*

Servants, Officers, Captain, Herald, Gentlemen, Soldiers, Musicians, Lords, Ladies, and Attendants

SOURCES

The sources for this play are William Shakespeare's Love's Labour's Lost (1595-6) and The Tragedy of King Lear (1605-6).

The author is indebted to the invaluable online resources of MIT's Shakespeare website (http://shakespeare.mit.edu/) and the Complete Moby™ Shakespeare.

NOTES ON THE TEXT

Every effort was made to preserve the rhythm, language and poetry of the original sources, particularly in the verse sections of the play.

A certain amount of rewording is necessary as a practical matter of fusing the two texts. For example, combining the role of the King of France (Lear) with the Princess of France (LLL) requires that numerous instances of "he" be replaced with "she," and "him" with "her," etc.

Whenever possible, replacement text is matched syllable-for-syllable. Thus, in verse sections, "man" might be replaced with "maid," rather than "woman," to preserve the meter.

Always, the objective is to ensure that the original rhyme scheme, pronunciation and operative words are not inadvertently affected by modifications in the storyline.

DOUBLING OF ROLES

In Elizabethan and Jacobean England, it was illegal for women to appear upon the public stage. Hence, the plays of Shakespeare were written to be performed by an all-male company of actors with only a handful of female characters—largely secondary roles played by boys.

These male-heavy casts present a challenge in modern-day stagings, where acting companies usually consist of a more balanced troupe of men and women. To accommodate this, gender-blind casting[1] is recommended for the plays of Shakespeare, as well as gender-reversal[2], to adapt the plays to the available talent pool.

The following breakdown for this play yields an abbreviated cast of twelve actors—six men, six women:

MALE	FEMALE
KING LEAR	**PRINCESS OF FRANCE**
COSTARD	**GONERIL**
KENT	**REGAN**
GLOUCESTER	**CORDELIA**
EDMUND	**JAQUENETTA**
EDGAR	**BOYET**

---

[1] Casting the best actor for the part, regardless of their gender.
[2] Changing the sex of the character to fit the actor who will be playing the part.

ABOUT THE AUTHORS

William Shakespeare is an English poet and playwright, generally regarded as the greatest writer in the English language, and by many as the greatest dramatist in history. His extant work includes 37 plays, 154 sonnets, and a number of other poems and collaborations. His plays have been translated into virtually every language and performed throughout the world.

Jeff Goode is an American director, playwright and screenwriter. He is the creator of the Disney Channel's animated series *American Dragon: Jake Long*, and the author of over 50 plays and musicals, including *The Eight: Reindeer Monologues*.

NEW PLAYS BY WILLIAM SHAKESPEARE
& JEFF GOODE:
Romeo & Julius [Caesar]
Ham/thello: the Moor of Denmark
Lear's Labour's Lost

ACT I - Vowers & Dowers

SCENE 1 - King Lear's palace.

(Enter **KENT** *and* **GLOUCESTER**.*)*

GLOUCESTER
Why the King of France is so suddenly gone back know you the reason?

KENT
Something he left imperfect in the state, that his personal return was most required and necessary.

GLOUCESTER
Who hath he left behind him general?

KENT
The Princess of France, his daughter heir,
A maid of grace and complete majesty—
For well you know she comes in embassy
On serious business, with the king to speak
About surrender up of Aquitaine.

GLOUCESTER
You are not ignorant, all-telling fame
Doth noise abroad, that Lear hath made a vow,
Till painful study shall outwear three years,
No woman may approach his silent court.

KENT
The trick of that vow I do well remember.

GLOUCESTER
Else your memory is bad.

KENT
But who comes here?

(Enter **EDMUND**.*)*

EDMUND

This letter, father, craves a speedy answer;
'Tis from the country servant Jaquenetta.

GLOUCESTER

O, thy letter, thy letter! she's a good friend of mine.

(Takes the letter.)

Do you know this noble gentleman, Edmund?

EDMUND

No, my lord.

GLOUCESTER

My lord of Kent: remember him hereafter as my honourable friend.

EDMUND

My services to your lordship.

KENT

Is not this your son, my lord?

GLOUCESTER

His breeding, sir, hath been at my charge: I have so often blushed to acknowledge him, that now I am brazed to it.

KENT

I cannot conceive you.

GLOUCESTER

Sir, this young fellow's mother could: whereupon she grew round-wombed, and had, indeed, sir, a son for her cradle ere she had a husband for her bed. Do you smell a fault?

KENT

I cannot wish the fault undone, the issue of it being so proper.

GLOUCESTER

Though this knave came something saucily into the world before he was sent for, yet was his mother fair; there was good sport at his making, and the whoreson must be acknowledged. But I have, sir, a son by order of law, some year elder than this, who yet is no dearer in my account,—

EDMUND

My brother Edgar.

GLOUCESTER

And his troth plight,
That he would wed the one or else the other
Of King Lear's eldest daughters.

KENT

I thought your son had more affected the Princess Goneril than Regan.

GLOUCESTER

It did always seem so to us: but now, in the division of his affection, it appears not which of the two he values most.

EDMUND

But what to me, my lord? but what to me? A wife?

GLOUCESTER

Your wife, so I would say, shall be Cordelia,
The younger daughter of our noble king.

EDMUND

[Aside] Whose daughters profit very greatly under him.

(**GLOUCESTER** *gives him a jewel pouch.*)

GLOUCESTER

If you will marry, ope this purse, and take
What it contains. If you shall see Cordelia,—
As fear not but you shall,—show her this ring;
And to her sweet hand see thou do commend it;
And she will tell you who your fortune is
If yet you do not know.

EDMUND

                                She is a jewel
Well worth a poor man's taking: fairies and gods,
A wife of such means were felicity.

(*Exit. Sennet.*)

GLOUCESTER

The king is coming.

*(Enter **KING LEAR**, **COSTARD** the king's fool, and Attendants.)*

KING LEAR

Our late edict shall strongly stand in force:
Navarre shall be the wonder of the world;
Our court shall be a little Academe,
Still and contemplative in living art.
You three, Lord Kent, Lord Gloucester, and the fool,—

COSTARD

Your servant, and Costard.

KING LEAR

Have sworn for three years' term to live with me,
My fellow-scholars, and to keep those statutes
That are recorded in this schedule here:

(Presents a proclamation for them to sign.)

If you are arm'd to do as sworn to do,
Subscribe to your deep oaths, and keep it too.

KENT

So much, dear liege, I have already sworn,
That is, to live and study here three years.
But there are other strict observances;
As, not to see a woman in that term,
Which I hope well is not enrollèd there;
And one day in a week to touch no food,
And then, to sleep but three hours in the night,
And not be seen to wink of all the day—
O, these are barren tasks, too hard to keep,
Not to see ladies, study, fast, not sleep!

KING LEAR

Your oath is pass'd to pass away from these.

KENT

Let me say no, my liege, an if you please:
I only swore to study with your grace
And stay here in your court for three years' space.

KING LEAR

You swore to that, Lord Kent, and to the rest.

KENT

> By yea and nay, sir, then I swore in jest.

KING LEAR

> Hear me, recreant; on thine allegiance, hear me!
> Since thou hast sought to make us break our vow,
> Which we durst never yet, take thy reward.
> Five days we do allot thee, for provision
> To shield thee from diseases of the world;
> And on the sixth to turn thy hated back
> Upon our kingdom: if, on the tenth day following,
> Thy banish'd trunk be found in our dominions,
> The moment is thy death. Away! by Jupiter,
> This shall not be revoked.

KENT

>   But good my liege,—

KING LEAR

> Bid me farewell, and let me hear thee going.

   (Storms out.)

KENT

> Nay, then will I be gone.

   (Withdraws.)

GLOUCESTER

> Kent banish'd thus! the king in choler parted!
> Navarre become a cloister! All this done
> Upon the gad!

COSTARD

> I'll lay my head to any good man's hat,
> These oaths and laws will prove an idle scorn.

   *(Re-enter **KING LEAR**.)*

KING LEAR

> Well, sit you out, as well: go home: adieu.

GLOUCESTER

> No, my good lord; we have sworn to stay with you:
> Give me the paper; let me read the same;
> And to the strict'st decrees I'll write my name.

KING LEAR

How well this yielding rescues thee from shame!

GLOUCESTER

I am resolved; 'tis but a three years' fast:
The mind shall banquet, though the body pine.

(Subscribes.)

KING LEAR

[To **COSTARD***]* What says my fellow?

COSTARD

My loving lord, thy fool is mortified:
The grosser manner of these world's delights
He throws upon the gross world's baser slaves:
To love, to wealth, to pomp, I pine and die;
With all these living in philosophy.
So to the laws at large I write my name.

(Subscribes.)

KING LEAR

And he that breaks them in the least degree
Stands in attainder of eternal shame.

(Re-enter **KENT** *above, unseen by those below.)*

GLOUCESTER

[Reads] 'Item, If any woman shall come within a mile of my court: she shall endure such public shame as the rest of the court can possibly devise.'
This article, my liege, yourself must break;
Your daughters come to sojourn at your house;—

KING LEAR

But yet they are my flesh, my blood, my daughters.

GLOUCESTER

As well, the daughter of the King of France
Importunes personal conference with your grace:
Therefore this article is made in vain,
Or vainly comes the admirèd princess hither.

KING LEAR

What say you, lords? Why, this was quite forgot.

KENT

> *[Aside]* So study evermore is overshot:
> While it doth study to have what it would
> It doth forget to do the thing it should.

KING LEAR

> We must of force dispense with this decree;
> She must lie here on mere necessity.
> Therefore to's seemeth it a needful course,
> Before she enter these forbidden gates,
> To know her pleasure; and in that behalf,
> Haste, signify so much; we will attend.

> *(Exeunt all but* **KENT**.*)*

KENT

> Necessity will make us all forsworn
> Three thousand times within this three years' space;
> If I break faith, this word shall speak for me;
> I am forsworn on 'mere necessity.'

> *(Subscribes.)*

> Suggestions are to other as to me;
> But I believe, although I seem so loath,
> I am the last that will last keep his oath.

> *(Disguises himself.)*

> If but as well I other accents borrow,
> That can my speech defuse, my good intent
> May carry through itself to that full issue
> For which I razed my likeness. Now, banish'd Kent,
> If thou canst serve where thou dost stand condemn'd,
> So may it come, thy master, whom thou lovest,
> Shall find thee full of labours.

> *(Exit.)*

SCENE 2 - The king's park.

(Enter the **PRINCESS** *of France, Ladies, and other Attendants.)*

LADY

Consider who the king your father sends,
To whom he sends, and what's his embassy:
Yourself, held precious in the world's esteem,
To parley with the sole inheritor
Of all perfections that a man may owe,
Matchless King Lear; the plea of no less weight
Than Aquitaine, a dowry for a queen.

PRINCESS

Here comes Boyet, and mirth is in her face.

(Enter **BOYET**.*)*

BOYET

O, I am stabb'd with laughter! Where's her grace?

PRINCESS

Thy news, Boyet? Now, what admittance, lady?

BOYET

The king had notice of your fair approach
Before I came. Marry, thus much I have learnt:
He rather means to lodge you in the field,
Like one that comes here to besiege his court,
Than seek a dispensation for his oath,
To let you enter his unpeopled house.

LADY

Here comes King Lear.

(Enter **KING LEAR**, **GLOUCESTER**, **COSTARD**, *and the king's daughters,* **GONERIL**, **REGAN**, **CORDELIA**, *and Attendants, among them,* **JAQUENETTA**, *and* **KENT**, *disguised.)*

KING LEAR

Fair princess, welcome to the court of Navarre.

PRINCESS

'Fair' I give you back again; and 'welcome' I have not

yet: the roof of this court is too high to be yours; and welcome to the wide fields too base to be mine.

KING LEAR

You shall be welcome, madam, to my court.

PRINCESS

I will be welcome, then: conduct me thither.

KING LEAR

Hear me, dear lady; I have sworn an oath.

PRINCESS

Our Lady help my lord! he'll be forsworn.

KING LEAR

Not for the world, fair madam, by my will.

PRINCESS

Why, will shall break it; will and nothing else.

KING LEAR

Your ladyship is ignorant what it is.

PRINCESS

I hear your grace hath sworn out house-keeping:
'Tis deadly sin to keep that oath, my lord,
And sin to break it.
But pardon me. I am too sudden-bold:
To teach a teacher ill beseemeth me.

(Handing him a letter.)

Vouchsafe to read the purpose of my coming,
And suddenly resolve me in my suit.

KING LEAR

Madam, I will, if suddenly I may.

PRINCESS

You will the sooner, that I were away;
For you'll prove perjured if you make me stay.

*(**KING LEAR** reads over the letter.)*

KING LEAR

Madam, your father here doth intimate
The payment of a hundred thousand crowns,
To have his title live in Aquitaine.
I do protest I never heard of it;

And if you prove it, I'll repay it back
Or yield up Aquitaine.
PRINCESS
                        We arrest your word.
Boyet, you can produce acquittances.
BOYET
To-morrow you shall have a sight of them.
KING LEAR
It shall suffice me: at which interview
All liberal reason I will yield unto.
Meantime we shall express our darker purpose.
Give me the map there. Know that we have divided
In three our kingdom: and 'tis our fast intent
To shake all cares and business of our state,—
These be the stops that hinder study quite—
Conferring them on younger strengths, while we
Unburthen'd pore on books. Belovèd Regan,
And you, our no less loving Princess Goneril,
Cordelia last, but not the least in love,
We have this hour a constant will to publish
Our daughters' several dowers, that future strife
May be prevented now.
The sons of Gloucester, Edgar and his brother,
Great rivals in our several daughters' love,
Long in our court have made their amorous sojourn,
And here are to be answer'd. Call them forth.

(An Attendant exits.)

COSTARD
[Aside to **GLOUCESTER***]* Sir, I pray you, a word: what lady is that same?
GLOUCESTER
The heir of royal Lear, Regan is her name.
COSTARD
Is she wedded or no?
GLOUCESTER
To her will, sir, or so.

*(***COSTARD*** starts toward* **REGAN***, but comes back.)*

COSTARD
What's her name in the cap?
GLOUCESTER
She is the Princess Goneril.
COSTARD
She is a most sweet lady.
GLOUCESTER
Not unlike, sir, that may be.

>   (**COSTARD** *starts toward* **GONERIL**, *but comes back.*)

COSTARD
Who are the rest?
GLOUCESTER
Peace, sirrah!
KENT
[Aside to **CORDELIA***]* Did not I dance with you in Brabant once?
CORDELIA
Did not I dance with you in Brabant once?
KENT
I know you did.
CORDELIA
How needless was it then to ask the question!
KENT
You must not be so quick.
CORDELIA
'Tis 'long of you that spur me with such questions.
KENT
Your wit's too hot, it speeds too fast, 'twill tire.
CORDELIA
Not till it leave the rider in the mire.

>   *(Withdraws.)*

KENT
[Aside] Woman of sovereign parts she is esteem'd;
Well fitted in arts, glorious in arms:
Nothing becomes her ill that she would well.
The only soil of her fair virtue's gloss,

If virtue's gloss will stain with any soil,
Is a sharp wit matched with too blunt a will.
   (Withdraws.)

KING LEAR

Tell me, my daughters,—
Since now we will divest us both of rule,
Interest of territory, cares of state,—
Which of you shall we say doth love us most?
That we our largest bounty may extend
Where nature doth with merit challenge.
Goneril, our eldest-born, speak first.

GONERIL

Sir, I love you more than words can wield the matter;
Dearer than eye-sight, space, and liberty;
Beyond what can be valued, rich or rare;
No less than life, with grace, health, beauty, honour;
As much as child e'er loved, or father found;
A love that makes breath poor, and speech unable;
Beyond all manner of so much I love you.

COSTARD

[Aside] Her eye begets occasion for her wit;
So sweet and voluble is her discourse.

LEAR

Of all these bounds, even from this line to this,
We make thee lady: to thee and thine issue
Be this perpetual.

CORDELIA

[Aside] What shall Cordelia do? Love, and be silent.

LEAR

What says our second daughter,
Our dearest Regan, plight to Edgar? Speak.

REGAN

I am made of that self mettle as my sister,
And prize me at her worth. In my true heart
I find she names my very deed of love;
Only she comes too short: that I profess
Myself an enemy to all other joys,

Which the most precious square of sense possesses;
And find I am alone felicitate
In your dear highness' love.

COSTARD

[Aside] O she hath wit to make an ill shape good,
And shape to win grace though she had no wit.

KING LEAR

To thee and thine hereditary ever
Remain this ample third of our fair kingdom;
No less in space, validity, and pleasure,
Than that conferr'd on Goneril.

CORDELIA

[Aside] Then poor Cordelia!
And yet not so; since, I am sure, my love's
More richer than my tongue.

> (**COSTARD** *takes* **REGAN** *aside, kisses her hand.*)

COSTARD

Lady, I will commend you to mine own heart.

REGAN

Pray you, do my commendations; I would be glad to see it.

COSTARD

I would you heard it groan.

GONERIL

[Overhearing] Is the fool sick?

COSTARD

Sick at the heart.

GONERIL

Alack, let it blood.

COSTARD

Would that do it good?

REGAN

My physic says 'ay.'

COSTARD

Will you prick't with your eye?

GONERIL

No point, with my knife.

REGAN
Now, God save thy life!
COSTARD
Do you hear, my mad wenches?
GONERIL
No.
COSTARD
What then, do you see?
REGAN
Ay, our way to be gone.
COSTARD
You are too hard for me.
  (Withdraws.)
REGAN
Good sir, be not offended.
GLOUCESTER
By my soul, a swain! a most simple clown!
Lord, Lord, how the ladies have both put him down!
  (Enter **EDGAR**.*)*
EDGAR
Well bandied both; a set of wit well play'd.
REGAN
Welcome, pure wit! thou partest a fair fray.
EDGAR
O, let me kiss that hand!
REGAN
Let me wipe it first; it smells of mortality.
COSTARD
[Aside to **JAQUENETTA***]* The tongues of mocking wenches are as keen
As is the razor's edge invisible,
Whose edge hath power to cut, whose will still wills
It should none spare that come within their power.
JAQUENETTA
Lord, how wise you are!

COSTARD

Think you so? Your name, fair gentlewoman?

JAQUENETTA

Jaquenetta, by good hap.

COSTARD

Give me your hand: away! the gentles are at their game, and we will to our recreation.

(Exeunt **COSTARD** *and* **JAQUENETTA**.*)*

KING LEAR

Now, our joy,
Although the last, not least; to whose young love
The bastard son of Gloucester, Edmund doth
Strive to be interess'd; what can you say to draw
A third more opulent than your sisters? Speak.

CORDELIA

Nothing, my lord.

KING LEAR

Nothing!

CORDELIA

Nothing.

KING LEAR

Nothing will come of nothing: speak again.

CORDELIA

Unhappy that I am, I cannot heave
My heart into my mouth: I love your majesty
According to my bond; nor more nor less.

KING LEAR

How, how, Cordelia! mend your speech a little,
Lest it may mar your fortunes.

CORDELIA

                        Good my lord,
You have begot me, bred me, loved me: I
Return those duties back as are right fit,
Obey you, love you, and most honour you.
How shall my sisters husband, if they say
They love you all? Haply, when I shall wed,
That lord whose hand must take my plight shall carry

Half my love with him, half my care and duty:
Sure I shall never wed if, like my sisters,
I loved my father all.

KING LEAR

But goes thy heart with this?

CORDELIA

                                    Ay, good my lord.

KING LEAR

So young, and so untender?

CORDELIA

So young, my lord, and true.

KING LEAR

Let it be so; thy truth, then, be thy dower:
For, by the sacred radiance of the sun,
Here I disclaim all my paternal care,
Propinquity and property of blood,
And as a stranger to my heart and me
Hold thee, from this, for ever.

KENT

                                  Good my liege,—

KING LEAR

Peace, knave!
Come not between the dragon and his wrath.
I loved her most, and thought to set my rest
On her kind nursery. Hence, and avoid my sight!
So be my grave my peace, as here I give
Her father's heart from her!
Call Edmund forth. Regan and Goneril,
With thy two divers dowers digest this third:
Let pride, which she calls plainness, marry her.
I do invest you jointly with my power,
Pre-eminence, and all the large effects
That troop with majesty. Ourself, by monthly course,
With reservation of an hundred knights,
By you to be sustain'd, shall our abode
Make with you by due turns. Only we still retain
The name, and all the additions to a king;
The sway, revenue, execution of the realm,

Belovèd ones, be yours: which to confirm,
This coronet part betwixt you.
   (Giving the crown.)

KENT
                        Royal Lear,
Whom I have ever honour'd as my king,
Loved as my father, as my master follow'd,—

KING LEAR
The bow is bent and drawn, make from the shaft.

KENT
Think'st thou that duty shall have dread to speak,
When power to flattery bows? To plainness honour's bound,
When majesty stoops to folly. Reverse thy doom:
Thy youngest daughter does not love thee least;
Nor are those empty-hearted whose low sound
Reverbs no hollowness.

KING LEAR
Knave, on thy life, no more.

KENT
My life I never held but as a pawn
To wage against thy enemies; nor fear to lose it,
Thy safety being the motive.

KING LEAR
                        Who are you?
Mine eyes are not o' the best: I'll tell you straight.
This is a dull sight. Are you not Kent?

KENT
                                The same,
Your servant Kent, my lord.

KING LEAR
                        Out of my sight!

KENT
See better, Lear; and let me still remain.

KING LEAR
O, vassal! miscreant!
   (Drawing his sword.)

GLOUCESTER

                    Dear sir, forbear.

KENT

                               Do:
Kill thy physician, and the fee bestow
Upon thy foul disease. Revoke thy doom;
Or, whilst I can vent clamour from my throat,
I'll tell thee thou dost evil.

KING LEAR

Take away this villain; shut him up.

GLOUCESTER

Come, you transgressing slave; away!

KENT

Fare thee well, king: sith thus thou wilt appear,
Freedom lives hence, and banishment is here.
[To **CORDELIA***]* The gods to their dear shelter take thee, maid,
That justly think'st, and hast most rightly said!
[To **REGAN** *and* **GONERIL***]* And your large speeches may your deeds approve,
That good effects may spring from words of love.
Thus Kent, O princes, bids you all adieu;
He'll shape his old course in a country new.

    (*Exeunt* **KENT** *and* **GLOUCESTER**.)

GONERIL

This Kent is like an envious sneaping frost,
That bites the first-born infants of the spring.

REGAN

The fellow pecks up wit as pigeons pease,
And utters it again when God doth please.

    (*Enter* **EDMUND**.)

EDMUND

Here's Edmund, noble lord. What is your will?

KING LEAR

My lord of Gloucester's son, who with your love
Hath rivall'd for our daughter: what, in the least,

Will you require in present dower with her,
Or cease your quest of love?

EDMUND
                          Most royal majesty.
I crave no more than what your highness offer'd,
Nor will you tender less.

KING LEAR
                          Right noble Edmund, list,
When she was dear to us, we did hold her so;
But now her price is fall'n. Sir, there she stands:
If aught within that little seeming substance,
And nothing more, may fitly like your grace,
She's there, and she is yours.

EDMUND
                          I know no answer.

KING LEAR
Will you, with those infirmities she owes,
Unfriended, new-adopted to our hate,
Dower'd with our curse, and stranger'd with our oath,
Take her, or leave her?

EDMUND
                          Pardon me, royal sir;
Election makes not up on such conditions.

KING LEAR
Then leave her, sir; for, by the power that made me,
I tell you all her wealth.

PRINCESS
                          This is most strange,
That she, that even but now was your best object,
The argument of your praise, balm of your age,
Most best, most dearest, should in this trice of time
Commit a thing so monstrous, to dismantle
So many folds of favour. Sure, her offence
Must be of such unnatural degree,
That monsters it.

CORDELIA
It is no vicious blot, murder, or foulness,
But even for want of that for which I am richer,

A still-soliciting eye, and such a tongue
As I am glad I have not, though not to have it
Hath lost me in your liking.

KING LEAR

            Better thou
Hadst not been born than not to have pleased me
better.

PRINCESS

Is it but this,—a tardiness in nature
Which often leaves the history unspoke
That it intends to do? My lord of Gloucester's son,
What say you to the lady? Love's not love
When it is mingled with regards that stand
Aloof from the entire point. Will you have her?
She is herself a dowry.

EDMUND

         Royal Lear,
Give but that portion which yourself proposed,
And here I take Cordelia by the hand,
Dowered so bountifully.

KING LEAR

            Nothing: I have sworn; I am firm.

EDMUND

I am sorry, then, you have so lost a father
That you must lose a husband.

CORDELIA

Peace be with Edmund, then!
Since that respects of fortune are his love,
I shall not be his wife.

KING LEAR

           For you, great France,
I would not from your love make such a stray,
To friend you where I hate; therefore beseech you
To avert your liking a more worthier way
Than on a wretch whom nature is ashamed
Almost to acknowledge hers.

PRINCESS

Fairest Cordelia, that art most rich, being poor,

Most choice, forsaken; and most loved, despised!
Thee and thy virtues here I seize upon.

CORDELIA

I am thankful for it.

PRINCESS

Be it lawful I take up what's cast away.
Thy dowerless daughter, king, thrown to my chance,
Is one of us, of ours, and our fair France:
Not all the Earl of Gloucester's bastard sons
Can buy this unprized precious maid of me.
Bid them farewell, Cordelia, though unkind:
Thou losest here, a better where to find.

KING LEAR

Thou hast her, France: let her be thine; for we
Have no such daughter, nor shall ever see
That face of hers again. Therefore be gone
Without our grace, our love, our benison.
Come, noble Edmund, come.
Dinner, ho, dinner! Where's my knave? my fool? Go you, and call my fool hither.

(Enter **GLOUCESTER** *with* **COSTARD** *and* **JAQUENETTA**, *in custody.)*

GLOUCESTER

Where is the king's own person?

KING LEAR

Here, Gloucester: what wouldst?

GLOUCESTER

There's villainy abroad: this coxcomb will tell you more. Let him confess and turn it to a jest.

COSTARD

Sir, the contempts thereof are as touching me. The matter is to me, sir, as concerning Jaquenetta. The manner of it is, I was taken with the manner.

KING LEAR

In what manner?

COSTARD

In manner and form following, sir; all those three: I

was seen with her in the manor-house, sitting with her upon the form, and taken following her into the park; which, put together, is in manner and form following.

GLOUCESTER

There did I see that low-spirited swain, that base minnow of thy mirth,—

COSTARD

With a wench.

GLOUCESTER

With a child of our grandmother Eve, a female; or, for thy more sweet understanding, a woman. Him I, as my ever-esteemed duty pricks me on, have brought to thee, to receive the meed of punishment. For Jaquenetta,— so is the weaker vessel called which I apprehended with the aforesaid swain,—I keep her as a vessel of the law's fury; and shall, at the least of thy sweet notice, bring her to trial.

KING LEAR

But, sirrah, what say you to this?

COSTARD

Sir, I confess the wench.

KING LEAR

Did you hear the proclamation?

COSTARD

I do confess much of the hearing it but little of the marking of it.

KING LEAR

It was proclaimed a year's imprisonment, to be taken with a wench.

COSTARD

I was taken with none, sir: I was taken with a damsel.

KING LEAR

Well, it was proclaimed 'damsel.'

COSTARD

This was no damsel, neither, sir; she was a virgin.

KING LEAR

It is so varied, too; for it was proclaimed 'virgin.'

COSTARD

If it were, I deny her virginity: I was taken with a maid.

KING LEAR

Sir, I will pronounce your sentence: you shall fast a week with bran and water.

COSTARD

I had rather pray a month with mutton and porridge.

KING LEAR

And Lord of Gloucester shall be your keeper.
And go we, lords, to put in practise that
Which each to other hath so strongly sworn.

(*Exeunt* **KING LEAR**, **EDMUND**, **EDGAR** *and Attendants.*)

COSTARD

I suffer for the truth, sir; for true it is, I was taken with Jaquenetta, and Jaquenetta is a true girl; and therefore welcome the sour cup of prosperity! Affliction may one day smile again; and till then, sit thee down, sorrow!

GLOUCESTER

Sirrah, come on.

(*Exeunt* **GLOUCESTER**, **COSTARD** *and* **JAQUENETTA**.)

PRINCESS

Bid farewell to your sisters.

CORDELIA

The jewels of our father, with wash'd eyes
Cordelia leaves you: I know you what you are;
And like a sister am most loath to call
Your faults as they are named. Use well our father.

REGAN

Prescribe not us our duties.

GONERIL

                                    Let your study
Be to content her grace, who hath received you
At fortune's alms. You have obedience scanted,
And well are worth the want that you have wanted.

CORDELIA

Time shall unfold what plaited cunning hides:

Who cover faults, at last shame them derides.
Well may you prosper!

PRINCESS

                        Come, my fair Cordelia.

(Exeunt **PRINCESS**, **CORDELIA**, **BOYET**, *and Attendants.)*

GONERIL

Sister, it is not a little I have to say of what most nearly appertains to us both. I think our father will hence to-night.

REGAN

That's most certain, and with you; next month with us.

GONERIL

You see how full of changes his age is; the observation we have made of it hath not been little: he always loved our sister most; and with what poor judgment he hath now cast her off appears too grossly.

REGAN

Such unconstant starts are we like to have from him as this of Kent's banishment.

GONERIL

There is further compliment of leavetaking between France and him. Pray you, let's hit together: if our father carry authority with such dispositions as he bears, this last surrender of his will but offend us.

REGAN

We shall further think on't.

GONERIL

We must do something, and i' the heat.

    (Exeunt.)

End of Act I

ACT II - Baseborn & Forsworn

SCENE 1 - The king's park.

(Enter **GLOUCESTER, COSTARD, JAQUENETTA** *and* **EDMUND**.*)*

GLOUCESTER
Villain, thou shalt fast for thy offences ere thou be pardoned.
COSTARD
Let me not be pent up, sir: I will fast, being loose.
GLOUCESTER
No, sir; that were fast and loose: thou shalt to prison.
(Enter **GONERIL**.*)*
GONERIL
Sir, the king's pleasure is, that you keep Costard safe: and you must suffer him to take no delight nor no penance; but a' must fast three days a week. For this damsel, I must keep her at the park: she is allowed for the day-woman.
JAQUENETTA
Fare you well.
GLOUCESTER
I do betray myself with blushing. Maid!
JAQUENETTA
Man?
GLOUCESTER
I love thee.
GONERIL
Come, Jaquenetta, away!
JAQUENETTA
Fair weather after you!

(Exeunt **GONERIL** *and* **JAQUENETTA**.*)*

GLOUCESTER
Fool, what sign is it when a man of great spirit grows melancholy?

COSTARD
A great sign, sir, that he will look sad.

GLOUCESTER
[To **EDMUND***]* Boy, I do love that country girl that I took in the park with the rational hind Costard.

EDMUND
So I heard you say.

GLOUCESTER
Sirrah Costard, I will enfranchise thee. I give thee thy liberty, set thee from durance; and, in lieu thereof, impose on thee nothing but this:

(Giving a letter.)

bear this significant to the country maid Jaquenetta: there is remuneration; for the best ward of mine honour is rewarding my dependents. Son, follow.

(Exit.)

EDMUND
[Aside] This maid will not serve your turn, sir.
This maid will serve my turn, sir.

(Exit.)

COSTARD
Now will I look to his remuneration. Remuneration! why, it is a fairer name than French crown. I will never buy and sell out of this word.

(Enter **KENT**.*)*

KENT
O, my good knave Costard! exceedingly well met.
As thou wilt win my favour, good my knave,
Do one thing for me that I shall entreat.
The princess stays her camp here in the park,
And in her train there is a gentle lady;

When tongues speak sweetly, then they name her name,
Cordelia they call her: ask for her;
And with my services to her, deliver
This seal'd-up counsel. There's thy guerdon; go.

(Gives him a shilling, and exits.)

COSTARD
I will do it sir, in print. Gardon! Remuneration!

(Exit.)

SCENE 2 - The French camp.

(Enter **KING LEAR**, **PRINCESS**, **BOYET** *and Attendants.)*

KING LEAR
Meantime receive such welcome at my hand
As honour without breach of honour may
Make tender of to thy true worthiness:
You may not come, fair princess, in my gates;
But here without you shall be so received
As you shall deem yourself lodged in my heart,
Though so denied fair harbour in my house.
Your own good thoughts excuse me, and farewell:
To-morrow shall we visit you again.

BOYET
God give thee joy of him! the noble lord
Most honourably doth unhold his word.

PRINCESS
Boyet, prepare; I will away tonight.

KING LEAR
Madam, not so; I do beseech you, stay.

PRINCESS
You'll not be perjured, 'tis a hateful thing.
Prepare, I say. I thank you, gracious lord,
For my great suit so easily obtain'd.

(Exeunt all but **KING LEAR** *and* **OSWALD**, *a Steward.)*

KING LEAR
This is not generous, not gentle, not humble.

OSWALD
Thus pour the stars down plagues for perjury.

KING LEAR
Ha, ha! what sayest thou?

OSWALD
Nay, nothing, Master.

KING LEAR
What a brazen-faced varlet art thou—
(Beating him.)

OSWALD

    My lord, I am guiltless, as I am ignorant
    Of what hath moved you.

KING LEAR

    Take heed, sirrah; the whip.

OSWALD

    Help, ho! murder! help!

    (Exeunt.)

SCENE 3 - The Earl of Gloucester's castle.

(Enter **EDMUND**, *with a letter.)*

EDMUND

Thou, nature, art my goddess; to thy law
My services are bound. Wherefore should I
Stand in the plague of custom, and permit
The curiosity of nations to deprive me,
For that I am some twelve or fourteen moon-shines
Lag of a brother? Why bastard? wherefore base?
Who, in the lusty stealth of nature, take
More composition and fierce quality
Than doth, within a dull, stale, tired bed,
Go to the creating a whole tribe of fops,
Got 'tween asleep and wake? Well, then,
Legitimate Edgar, I must have your land:
Our father's love is to the bastard Edmund
As to the legitimate: fine word,—legitimate!
Well, my legitimate, if this letter speed,
And my invention thrive, Edmund the base
Shall top the legitimate. I grow; I prosper:
Now, gods, stand up for bastards!

(Enter **GLOUCESTER**.*)*

GLOUCESTER

Edmund, how now! what news?

EDMUND

So please your lordship, none.

(Hides the letter.)

GLOUCESTER

Why so earnestly seek you to put up that letter?

EDMUND

I beseech you, sir, pardon me: it is a letter from my brother, that I have not all o'er-read; and for so much as I have perused, I find it not fit for your o'er-looking.

GLOUCESTER

Give me the letter, sir.

EDMUND

I shall offend, either to detain or give it. The contents, as in part I understand them, are to blame.

GLOUCESTER

[Reads] 'I will hereupon confess I am in love: and as it is base for a soldier to love, so am I in love with a base wench—'

EDMUND

I hope, for my brother's justification, he wrote this but as an essay or taste of my virtue.

GLOUCESTER

[Reads] 'Come to me, that of this I may speak more. If our father would sleep till I waked him, I should enjoy Jaquenetta for ever, and you live the beloved of your brother, EDGAR.'
My son Edgar! Had he a hand to write this? a heart and brain to breed it in?

EDMUND

I dare pawn down my life for him, that he hath wrote this to feel my affection to your honour, and to no further pretence of danger.

GLOUCESTER

When came this to you? who brought it?

EDMUND

It was not brought me, my lord; there's the cunning of it; I found it thrown in at the casement of my closet.

GLOUCESTER

You know the character to be your brother's?

EDMUND

If the matter were good, my lord, I durst swear it were his; but, in respect of that, I would fain think it were not.

GLOUCESTER

It is his.

EDMUND

It is his hand, my lord; but I hope his heart is not in the contents.

GLOUCESTER

Hath he never heretofore sounded you in this business?

EDMUND

Never, my lord: but I have heard him oft maintain it that,
A wither'd hermit, five-score winters worn,
Might shake off fifty, looking in her eye.

GLOUCESTER

O villain, villain! His very opinion in the letter!
[Reads] 'Beauty doth varnish age, as if new-born,
And gives the crutch the cradle's infancy:—'
Abhorred villain! Where is he?

EDMUND

I do not well know, my lord.

GLOUCESTER

Edmund, seek him out: wind me into him, I pray you: frame the business after your own wisdom. I would unstate myself, to be in a due resolution.

EDMUND

I will seek him, sir, presently.

GLOUCESTER

And the noble and true-hearted Kent banished! his offence, honesty! 'Tis strange.

(Exit.)

EDMUND

And pat he comes like the catastrophe of the old comedy: my cue is villanous melancholy, with a sigh like Tom o' Bedlam. O!

(Enter **EDGAR**.*)*

EDGAR

How now, brother Edmund! what serious contemplation are you in?

EDMUND

Come, come; when saw you my father last?

EDGAR

Why, the night gone by.

EDMUND

Parted you in good terms? Found you no displeasure in him by word or countenance?

EDGAR

None at all.

EDMUND

Bethink yourself wherein you may have offended him: and at my entreaty forbear his presence till some little time hath qualified the heat of his displeasure; which at this instant so rageth in him, that with the mischief of your person it would scarcely allay.

EDGAR

Some villain hath done me wrong.

EDMUND

That's my fear. I pray you, retire with me to my lodging; there's my key: if you do stir abroad, go armed.

EDGAR

Armed, brother!

EDMUND

Brother, I advise you to the best; go armed: I am no honest man if there be any good meaning towards you: I pray you, away.

(Exit **EDGAR.** *)*

A credulous father! and a brother noble,
Whose nature is so far from doing harms,
That he suspects none: on whose foolish honesty
My practises ride easy! I see the business.
Let me, if not by birth, have lands by wit:
All with me's meet that I can fashion fit.

(Exit.)

SCENE 4 - The French camp.

(Enter the **PRINCESS**, **CORDELIA**, **BOYET** *and Attendants.)*

BOYET

Here comes a member of the commonwealth.

(Enter **COSTARD**.*)*

COSTARD

God dig-you-den all! Pray you, which is the head lady?

PRINCESS

Thou shalt know her, fellow, by the rest that have no heads.

COSTARD

Which is the greatest lady, the highest?

PRINCESS

The thickest and the tallest.

COSTARD

The thickest and the tallest! it is so; truth is truth.
Are not you the chief woman? you are the thickest here.

PRINCESS

What's your will, sir? what's your will?

COSTARD

I have a letter from Monsieur Lord Kent to one Lady Cordelia.

CORDELIA

Let's see, let's see.

PRINCESS

Who are the votaries, my good Boyet,
That are vow-fellows with this virtuous king?

BOYET

The Earl of Kent is one.

PRINCESS

[*To* **CORDELIA**] Know you the man?

CORDELIA

The young Lord Kent's a well-accomplished youth,

LEAR'S LABOUR'S LOST 45

Of all that virtue love for virtue loved:
Most power to do most harm, least knowing ill.
PRINCESS
Some merry mocking lord, belike; is't so?
CORDELIA
They say so most that most his humours know.
BOYET
Such short-lived wits do wither as they grow.
CORDELIA
But a merrier man,
Within the limit of becoming mirth,
I never spent an hour's talk withal:
For every object that his eye doth catch
His wit doth turn to a mirth-moving jest,
That agèd ears play truant at his tales
And younger hearings are quite ravishèd.
PRINCESS
God bless my lady! are you so in love,
That every fault of Kent hast garnishèd
With such bedecking ornaments of praise?
[To **COSTARD***]* Stand aside, good bearer. Boyet, you can carve;
Break up this capon.

> (Hands **BOYET** the letter.)

BOYET
       I am bound to serve.
This letter is mistook, it importeth none here;
It is writ to Jaquenetta.
PRINCESS
       We will read it, I swear.
Break the neck of the wax, and every one give ear.
BOYET
[Reads] 'Thus dost thou hear the Nemean lion roar
'Gainst thee, thou lamb, that standest as his prey.
Submissive fall his princely feet before,
And he from forage will incline to play:
But if thou strive, poor soul, what art thou then?

Food for his rage, repasture for his den.
Thine, in all compliments of devoted and heart-burning heat of duty, GLOUCESTER.'

PRINCESS
What plume of feathers is he that indited this letter?

BOYET
This Lord Gloucester is an old love-monger, that keeps here in court.

PRINCESS
Thou fellow, a word:
Who gave thee this letter?

COSTARD
I told you; my lord.

PRINCESS
To whom shouldst thou give it?

COSTARD
From my lord to my lady.

PRINCESS
From which lord to which lady?

COSTARD
From my lord of Kent, my good master's familiar,
To a lady of France that he called his Cordelia.

PRINCESS
Thou hast mistaken his letter. Come, let's, away.

COSTARD
I beseech you, pardon me, if I be mistaken—

PRINCESS
[To **CORDELIA***]* Here, sweet, put up this: 'twill be thine another day.

(*Exeunt* **PRINCESS** *and train.*)

COSTARD
Their several counsels have unbosom'd all
To loves mistook, I will be mock'd withal
Upon the next occasion that we meet,
With Gloucester and Lord Kent, to talk and greet.

(*Exit.*)

SCENE 5 - Goneril's chamber.

(Enter **GONERIL** *and* **JAQUENETTA**, *with a letter.)*

JAQUENETTA

Good mistress Princess, be so good as read me this letter: it was given me by Costard, and sent me from my lord Gloucester: I beseech you, read it.

GONERIL

What, my soul, verses?

JAQUENETTA

Ay, sooth, and very learned.
Let me hear a staff, a stanze, a verse.

GONERIL

[Reads] 'So sweet a kiss the golden sun gives not
To those fresh morning drops upon the rose,
As thy eye-beams, when their fresh rays have smote
The night of dew that on my cheeks down flows:—'
No more; the text is foolish.
But, damosella virgin, was this directed to you?

JAQUENETTA

Ay, sooth, from one Monsieur of Gloucester, one of the king's bookmates.

GONERIL

I will overglance the superscript: 'To the snow-white hand of the most beauteous Lady Cordelia.' I will look again for the party writing to the person written unto: 'Your ladyship's in all desired employment, KENT.' Jaquenetta, this Lord Kent is one of the votaries with the king; and here he hath framed a letter to my sister at the stranger queen's, which accidentally hath miscarried. Trip and go, my sweet; deliver this paper into the royal hand of the king: it may concern much. Stay not thy compliment; I forgive thy duty; adieu.

(Exeunt.)

SCENE 6 - The king's park.

(Enter **KENT**, *with a paper.)*

KENT

Am I, forsooth, in love! I, that have been love's whip;
A critic, nay, a night-watch constable;
A domineering pedant o'er the boy;
This senior-junior, giant-dwarf, Dan Cupid;
And I to be a corporal of his field,
And wear his colours like a tumbler's hoop!
Nay, to be perjured, which is worst of all;
And, among three, to love the worst of all;
Well, I do nothing in the world but lie, and lie in my throat. By heaven, I do love: and it hath taught me to rhyme and to be melancholy; and here is part of my rhyme, and here my melancholy. Well, she hath one o' my sonnets already: the clown bore it, the fool sent it, and the lady hath it: sweet clown, sweeter fool, sweetest lady! By the world, I would not care a pin, if the other three were in. Here comes one with a paper: God give him grace to groan!

*(**KENT** stands aside. Enter **KING LEAR**, with a paper.)*

KING LEAR

Ay me!

KENT

[Aside] Shot, by heaven! Proceed, sweet Cupid: thou hast thumped him with thy bird-bolt under the left pap. In faith, secrets!

KING LEAR

[Reads] 'O queen of queens! how far dost thou excel,
No thought can think, nor tongue of mortal tell.
Nor shines the silver moon one half so bright
Through the transparent bosom of the deep,
As doth thy face through tears of mine give light;
Thou shinest in every tear that I do weep:
No drop but as a coach doth carry thee;
So ridest thou triumphing in my woe.

Do but behold the tears that swell in me,
And they thy glory through my grief will show:
But do not love thyself; then thou wilt keep
My tears for glasses, and still make me weep.'
How shall she know my griefs? I'll drop the paper:
Sweet leaves, shade folly. Who is he comes here?

(Steps aside.)

What, Gloucester, too! and reading! listen, ear.

KENT

Now, in thy likeness, one more fool appear!

(Enter **GLOUCESTER**, *with a paper.)*

GLOUCESTER

Ay me, I am forsworn!

KENT

Why, he comes in like a perjure, wearing papers.

KING LEAR

In love, I hope: sweet fellowship in shame!

KENT

One drunkard loves another of the name.

GLOUCESTER

I do affect the very ground, which is base, where her shoe, which is baser, guided by her foot, which is basest, doth tread. I shall be forsworn, which is a great argument of falsehood, if I love. And how can that be true love which is falsely attempted? Love is a familiar; Love is a devil: there is no evil angel but Love. Assist me, some extemporal god of rhyme, for I am sure I shall turn sonnet. Devise, wit; write, pen; for I am for whole volumes in folio.
'O, but her eye,—by this light, but for her eye, I would not love her; yes, for her two eyes.'
O Jaquenetta, empress of my love!
I fear these stubborn lines lack power to move:
These numbers will I tear, and write in prose.
'Vows are but breath, and breath a vapour is:
Then thou, fair sun, which on my earth dost shine,
Exhalest this vapour-vow; in thee it is:

If broken then, it is no fault of mine:
If by me broke, what fool is not so wise
To lose an oath to win a paradise?'
By whom shall I send this?—Company! stay.
   (Steps aside.)

KENT
All hid, all hid; an old infant play.
Like a demigod here sit I in the sky.
And wretched fools' secrets heedfully o'ereye.
   (Enter **COSTARD**, *with a paper.)*

More sacks to the mill! O heavens, I have my wish!
The fool transform'd! four woodcocks in a dish!

COSTARD
O most divine Regan!

KENT
O most profane coxcomb!

COSTARD
Once more I'll read the ode that I have writ.

KENT
Once more I'll mark how love can vary wit.

COSTARD
[Reads] 'On a day—alack the day!—
Love, whose month is ever May,
Spied a blossom passing fair
Playing in the wanton air:
Air, quoth he, thy cheeks may blow;
Air, would I might triumph so!
But, alack, my hand is sworn
Ne'er to pluck thee from thy thorn;
Vow, alack, for youth unmeet,
Youth so apt to pluck a sweet!'
This will I send, and something else more plain,
That shall express my true love's fasting pain.
O, would the king, the earl, and banished Kent,
Were lovers too! Ill, to example ill,
Would from my forehead wipe a perjured note;
For none offend where all alike do dote.

But have I forgot my love Goneril?
Almost I had.
  (Takes out a second paper.)
Negligent student! learn her by heart.
By heart and in heart, fool.
And out of heart, coxcomb: all those three I will prove.
By, in, and without, upon the instant: by heart I love her, because my heart cannot come by her; in heart I love her, because my heart is in love with her; and out of heart I love her, being out of heart that I cannot enjoy her.
I am all these three.
And three times as much more, and yet nothing at all.
[Reads] 'Do not call it sin in me,
That I am forsworn for thee;
Thou for whom Jove would swear
Juno but an Ethiope were;
And deny himself for Jove,
Turning mortal for thy love.'

GLOUCESTER

  [Advancing] Costard, thy love is far from charity.
  You may look pale, but I should blush, I know,
  To be o'erheard and taken napping so.

KING LEAR

  [Advancing] Come, sir, you blush; as his your case is such;
  You chide at him, offending twice as much;
  I have been closely shrouded in this bush
  And mark'd you both and for you both did blush:
  I heard your guilty rhymes, observed your fashion,
  Saw sighs reek from you, noted well your passion.
  What would Lord Kent say if that he could hear
  Faith so infringèd, which such zeal did swear?
  He said it would be thus, poor banish'd man!
  How would he scorn! how would he spend his wit!
  How would he triumph, leap and laugh at it!
  For all the wealth that ever I did see,
  I would not have him know so much by me.

KENT
>Now step I forth to whip hypocrisy.
>*[Advancing]* Ah, good my liege, I pray thee, pardon me!
>Good heart, what grace hast thou, thus to reprove
>These worms for loving, that art most in love?
>Your eyes do make no coaches; in your tears
>There is no certain princess that appears.
>But are you not ashamed? nay, are you not,
>All three of you, to be thus much o'ershot?
>You found his mote; the king your mote did see;
>But I a beam do find in each of three.
>O, what a scene of foolery have I seen,
>Of sighs, of groans, of sorrow and of teen!
>O me, with what strict patience have I sat,
>To see a king transformèd to a gnat!

KING LEAR
>Are we betray'd thus to thy over-view?

KENT
>Not you to me, but I betray'd by you:
>I, that am honest; I, that hold it sin
>To break the vow I am engaged in;
>Kent, sir, the banish'd Kent; who in disguise
>Follow'd his enemy king, and did him service
>Improper for a slave;
>I am betray'd, by keeping company
>With men like men of inconstancy.
>When shall you see me write a thing in rhyme?
>Or groan for love? or spend a minute's time
>In pruning me? When shall you hear that I
>Will praise a hand, a foot, a face, an eye,
>
>>*(Sees* **JAQUENETTA** *coming and tries to flee.)*
>
>A gait, a state, a brow, a breast, a waist,
>A leg, a limb?

KING LEAR
>>Soft! whither away so fast?
>A true man or a thief that gallops so?

KENT
>I post from love: good lover, let me go.

(Enter **JAQUENETTA***.)*

JAQUENETTA
God bless the king!
KING LEAR
What present hast thou there?
JAQUENETTA
Some certain treason.
KING LEAR
What makes treason here?
JAQUENETTA
I beseech your grace, let this letter be read:
The princess misdoubts it; 'twas treason, she said.
KING LEAR
Good Kent, read it over.
(Giving him the paper.)
Where hadst thou it?
JAQUENETTA
Of Costard.
KING LEAR
Where hadst thou it?
COSTARD
Of Lord of Gloucester, sir, my lord of Gloucestershire.
*(***KENT** *tears the letter.)*

KING LEAR
How now! what is in you? why dost thou tear it?
KENT
A toy, my liege, a toy: your grace needs not fear it.
COSTARD
It did move him to passion, and therefore let's hear it.
GLOUCESTER
It is in Kent's writing, and here is his name.
KENT
[To **COSTARD***]* Ah, you whoreson loggerhead! you were born to do me shame.
Guilty, my lord, guilty! I confess, I confess.

KING LEAR
What?
KENT
That you three fools lack'd me fool to make up the mess:
He, he, and you, and you, my liege, and I,
Are pick-purses in love, and we deserve to die.
KING LEAR
What, did these rent lines show some love of thine?
KENT
Did they, quoth you? Who sees that sweet divine,
What peremptory eagle-sighted eye
Dares look upon Cordelia's heavenly brow,
That is not blinded by her majesty?
KING LEAR
What zeal, what fury hath inspired thee now?
My love, her mistress, is a gracious moon;
She an attending star, scarce seen a light.
KENT
My eyes are then no eyes, nor mid-day noon:
O, but for my love, day would turn to night!
KING LEAR
But what of this? are we not all in love?
KENT
Nothing so sure; and thereby all forsworn.
KING LEAR
Then leave this chat; and, good Sir Kent, now prove
Our loving lawful, and our faith not torn.
COSTARD
Ay, marry, there; some flattery for this evil.
GLOUCESTER
Some tricks, some quillets, how to cheat the devil.
KENT
Have at you, then, affection's men at arms.
Consider what you first did swear unto:—
COSTARD
To fast, to study, and to see no woman.

KENT

> O, we have made a vow to study, lords,
> And in that vow we have forsworn our books.
> For when would you, my liege, or you, or you,
> In leaden contemplation have found out
> Such fiery numbers as the prompting eyes
> Of beauty's tutors have enrich'd you with?
> From women's eyes this doctrine I derive:
> They are the books, the arts, the academes,
> From whence doth spring the true Promethean fire
> That show, contain and nourish all the world:
> Else none at all in ought proves excellent.

COSTARD

> Then fools we were these women to forswear.

GLOUCESTER

> Or keeping what is sworn, we will prove fools.

KENT

> Let us once lose our oaths to find ourselves,
> Or else we lose ourselves to keep our oaths.

KING LEAR

> Saint Cupid, then! and, soldiers, to the field!

KENT

> Advance your standards, and upon them, lords.

COSTARD

> Pell-mell, down with them! but be first advised,
> In conflict that you get the sun of them.

GLOUCESTER

> Shall we resolve to woo these girls, and France?

COSTARD

> And win them too: therefore let us devise
> Some entertainment for them in their tents.

KING LEAR

> First, from the park let us conduct them thither;
> Then homeward every man pursue the hand
> Of his fair mistress: in the afternoon
> We will with some strange pastime solace them.

KENT

>Away, away! no time shall be omitted
>That will betime, and may by us be fitted.

COSTARD

>Allons! allons! Sow'd cockle reap'd no corn:
>Light wenches may prove plagues to men forsworn.

>*(Exeunt all but **GLOUCESTER** and **JAQUENETTA**.)*

GLOUCESTER

>O, shall I say, I thank you, gentle wife?

JAQUENETTA

>Not so, my lord; until the judgment day
>I'll mark no words that smooth-faced wooers say.

GLOUCESTER

>Vows for thee broke deserve not punishment.
>A woman I forswore; but I will prove,
>Thou being a goddess, I forswore not thee:
>My vow was earthly, thou a heavenly love;
>Thy grace being gain'd cures all disgrace in me.

JAQUENETTA

>Come when the king doth to his lady come;
>Then, if I have much love, I'll give you some.

GLOUCESTER

>I'll serve thee true and faithfully till then.

JAQUENETTA

>Yet swear not, lest ye be forsworn again.

>*(Exeunt.)*

End of Act II

ACT III - Plighting & Fighting

SCENE 1 - The French camp.

(Enter **KING LEAR** *and* **KENT**.*)*

KING LEAR
Where's Boyet, ho? I think the world's asleep.
(Enter **BOYET**.*)*

BOYET
Fair sir, God save you!

KING LEAR
Where's the princess?

BOYET
Gone to her tent. Please it your majesty
Command me any service to her thither?

KING LEAR
That she vouchsafe me audience for one word.

BOYET
I will; and so will she, I know, my lord.
(Exit.)

KING LEAR
But how's my Kent? I have not seen thee this two days.

KENT
Since my young lady's going o'er to France, sir, thy Kent hath much pined away.

KING LEAR
No more of that; I have noted it well.
(Enter **OSWALD**.*)*
You, you, sirrah, where's my daughter?

OSWALD
So please you,—

KING LEAR

Prithee, if thou lovest me, tell me.

OSWALD

I love thee not.

(Exit.)

KING LEAR

What says the fellow there? Call the clotpoll back.

(Exit **KENT**.*)*

How now! where's that mongrel?

(Re-enter **KENT**.*)*

KENT

He says, my lord, your daughter is not well.

KING LEAR

Why came not the slave back to me when I called him?

KENT

Sir, he answered me in the roundest manner, he would not.

KING LEAR

He would not!

(Re-enter **OSWALD**.*)*

O, you sir, you, come you hither, sir: who am I, sir?

OSWALD

My lady's father.

KING LEAR

'My lady's father'! my lord's knave: you whoreson dog! you slave! you cur!

(Striking him.)

OSWALD

I'll not be struck, my lord.

KENT

Nor tripped neither, you base football player.

(Tripping up his heels.)

KING LEAR

Come, sir, arise, away! Go you, and tell my daughter I would speak with her.

(Exit **OSWALD**.*)*

KENT

My lord, I know not what the matter is; but, to my judgment, your highness is not entertained with that ceremonious affection as you were wont.

KING LEAR

Ha! sayest thou so?

(Enter the **PRINCESS** , **CORDELIA**, **BOYET**, *and Attendants.)*

All hail, sweet madam, and fair time of day!

PRINCESS

'Fair' in 'all hail' is foul, as I conceive.

KING LEAR

Construe my speeches better, if you may.

PRINCESS

Then wish me better; I will give you leave.

KING LEAR

We came to visit you, and purpose now
To lead you to our court; vouchsafe it then.

PRINCESS

This field shall hold me; and so hold your vow:
Nor God, nor I, delights in perjured men.

KING LEAR

Rebuke me not for that which you provoke:
The virtue of your eye must break my oath.

PRINCESS

You nickname virtue; vice you should have spoke;
For virtue's office never breaks men's troth.
Now by my maiden honour, yet as pure
As the unsullied lily, I protest,
A world of torments though I should endure,
I would not yield to be your house's guest;
So much I hate a breaking cause to be
Of heavenly oaths, vow'd with integrity.

KING LEAR

O undistinguish'd space of woman's will!

BOYET

It was well done of you to take him at his word.

PRINCESS

I was as willing to grapple as he was to board.

CORDELIA

Two hot sheeps, marry.

KENT

                              And wherefore not ships?
No sheep, sweet lamb, unless we feed on your lips.

CORDELIA

You sheep, and I pasture: shall that finish the jest?

KENT

So you grant pasture for me.

(Tries to kiss her.)

CORDELIA

                                 Not so, gentle beast:
My lips are no common, though several they be.

KENT

Belonging to whom?

CORDELIA

                           To my fortunes and me.

PRINCESS

Good wits will be jangling; but, gentles, agree:
This civil war of wits were much better used
By Navarre on his book-men; for here 'tis abused.
I'll not endure it.

KING LEAR

Doth any here know me? This is not Lear:
Doth Lear walk thus? speak thus? Where are his eyes?
Who is it that can tell me who I am?

PRINCESS

Lear's shadow.

KING LEAR

Detested kite! thou liest.

PRINCESS

You strike my people; and your disorder'd rabble
Make servants of their betters.

KING LEAR

Saddle my horses; call my train together:
Degenerate bastard! I'll not trouble thee.
No, do thy worst, blind Cupid! I'll not love.
Yet have I left my daughters.
Away! I have nothing to do with thee.
We'll no more meet, no more see one another:
But yet thou are a disease that's in my flesh,
A plague-sore, an embossèd carbuncle,
Which I must needs call mine. Prepare my horses!

(Exeunt **KING LEAR**, **KENT** *and Attendants.)*

BOYET

If my observation, which very seldom lies,
Deceive me not now, The king is infected
With that which we lovers entitle affected.
I'll give you Aquitaine and all that is his,
An you give him for my sake but one loving kiss.

PRINCESS

We will talk no more of this matter.
On Saturday we will return to France.

(Exeunt **PRINCESS** *and all her train, except* **CORDELIA** *and* **OSWALD**.*)*

CORDELIA

Whither is he going?

OSWALD

He calls to horse; but will I know not whither.

CORDELIA

What he hath utter'd I will write my sister.

OSWALD

I will commend your highness' letters to her.

(Exeunt.)

SCENE 2 - Gloucester's castle.

(Enter **EDMUND**.*)*

EDMUND

My father hath set guard to take my brother;
This weaves itself perforce into my business.
And I have one thing, of a queasy question,
Which I must act: briefness and fortune, work!
Brother, a word; descend: brother, I say!

(Enter **EDGAR**.*)*

My father watches: O sir, fly this place;
Intelligence is given where you are hid:
Have you not spoken 'gainst the Princess Regan?
He's coming hither: now, i' the night, i' the haste,
And Regan with him: have you nothing said
Upon his party 'gainst the Princess Goneril?
Advise yourself.

EDGAR

               I am sure on't, not a word.

EDMUND

I hear my father coming: pardon me:
In cunning I must draw my sword upon you
Draw; seem to defend yourself; now quit you well.
Yield: come before my father. Light, ho, here!
Fly, brother. Torches, torches! So, farewell.

(Exit **EDGAR**.*)*

Some blood drawn on me would beget opinion
Of my more fierce endeavour.

(Wounds his arm.)

                           I have seen drunkards
Do more than this in sport. Father, father!
Stop, stop! No help?

(Enter **GLOUCESTER**, *and Servants with torches.)*

GLOUCESTER

              Now, Edmund, where's the villain?

EDMUND
> Look, sir, I bleed.

GLOUCESTER
> Where is the villain, Edmund?

EDMUND
> Fled this way, sir. When by no means he could
> Persuade me to the murder of your lordship,
> Full suddenly he fled.

GLOUCESTER
> Let him fly far:
> Not in this land shall he remain uncaught.

EDMUND
> When I dissuaded him from his intent,
> And threaten'd to discover him: he replied,
> 'Thou unpossessing bastard! dost thou think,
> If I would stand against thee, would the reposal
> Of any trust, virtue, or worth in thee
> Make thy words faith'd? No: what I should deny,—'

GLOUCESTER
> Detested villain! Strong and fasten'd villain
> Would he deny his letter? I never got him.
> All ports I'll bar; the villain shall not 'scape;
> I will send far and near, that all the kingdom
> May have the due note of him;
> And found—dispatch. The noble king my master,
> By his authority I will proclaim it,
> That he which finds him shall deserve our thanks,
> He that conceals him, death; and of my land,
> Loyal and natural boy, I'll work the means
> To make thee capable.

> *(Tucket within.)*

> Hark, Regan's trumpets! I know not why she comes.

EDMUND
> Faith, the poor wench is cast away: she's quick; the child brags in her belly already: 'tis his.

GLOUCESTER

How!

EDMUND

She is two months on her way.

GLOUCESTER

Then shall Edgar be whipped for Princess Regan that is quick by him.

EDMUND

[Aside] And hanged for Gloucester that is dead to him.

(Enter **REGAN**, *and Attendants.)*

REGAN

If you do chance to hear of that blood traitor,
Preferment falls on him that cuts him off.
[To **GLOUCESTER***]* How now, my noble friend! since I came hither,
Which I can call but now, I have heard strange news.
If it be true, all vengeance comes too short
Which can pursue the offender. How dost, my lord?

GLOUCESTER

O, madam, my old heart is crack'd, it's crack'd!

REGAN

What, did my father's godson seek your life?
He whom my father named? your Edgar?

GLOUCESTER

O, lady, lady, shame would have it hid!

REGAN

Edmund, I hear that you have shown your father
A child-like office.

EDMUND

                          'Twas my duty, Princess.
Would I could meet him, madam! I should show
What party I do follow.

GLOUCESTER

He did bewray his practise; and received
This hurt you see, striving to apprehend him.

REGAN
> If he be taken, he shall never more
> Be fear'd of doing harm: make your own purpose,
> How in my strength you please. For you, Edmund,
> Whose virtue and obedience doth this instant
> So much commend itself, you shall be ours:
> Natures of such deep trust we shall much need;
> You we first seize on.

EDMUND
>   I shall serve your grace,
> Truly, however else.

GLOUCESTER
>   For him I thank your grace.

REGAN
> Take you some company, and away to horse:
> Inform my sister—

EDMUND
>   Regan, I bleed apace.

REGAN
> Untimely comes this hurt: give me your arm.

GLOUCESTER
> These late eclipses in the sun and moon portend no good to us: love cools, friendship falls off, brothers divide, and the bond cracked 'twixt son and father. This villain of mine comes under the prediction; there's son against father: the king falls from bias of nature; there's father against child. We have seen the best of our time: machinations, hollowness, treachery, and all ruinous disorders, follow us disquietly to our graves.

> *(Exit.)*

EDMUND
> Will you vouchsafe with me to change a word?

REGAN
> Name it.

EDMUND
>Fair lady,—

REGAN
>>Say you so? Fair lord,—
>Take that for your fair lady.

EDMUND
>>Please it you,
>As much in private, and I'll bid adieu.

>*(Exeunt.)*

SCENE 3 - A wood.

(Enter **EDGAR.***)*

EDGAR

I heard myself proclaim'd;
And by the happy hollow of a tree
Escaped the hunt. No port is free; no place,
That guard, and most unusual vigilance,
Does not attend my taking. Whiles I may 'scape,
I will preserve myself: and am bethought
To take the basest and most poorest shape
That ever penury, in contempt of man,
Brought near to beast: my face I'll grime with filth;
Blanket my loins: elf all my hair in knots.
The country gives me proof and precedent
Of Bedlam beggars, who, with roaring voices,
Enforce their charity. Poor Turlygod! poor Tom!
That's something yet: Edgar I nothing am.

(Exit.)

SCENE 4 - Before Goneril's castle.

(Enter **COSTARD** *and Musicians, serenading beneath Goneril's window.)*

COSTARD

[Sings] If love make me forsworn, how shall I swear to love?
Ah, never faith could hold, if not to beauty vow'd!
Though to myself forsworn, to thee I'll faithful prove:
Those thoughts to me were oaks, to thee like osiers bow'd.
Celestial as thou art, O, pardon, love, this wrong,
That sings heaven's praise with such an earthly tongue.

(Enter **GONERIL** *and* **EDMUND**.*)*

GONERIL

What would these strangers? know their minds, my lord.

EDMUND

What would you with the princess?

COSTARD

Nothing but peace and gentle visitation.

GONERIL

Why, that he has; and bid him so be gone.

EDMUND

She says, you have it, and you may be gone.

COSTARD

Say to her, I have measured many miles
To tread a measure with her on this grass.

GONERIL

Since you are strangers and come here by chance,
We'll not be nice: go to. We will not dance.

COSTARD

Be not as prodigal of all dear grace
As Nature was in making graces dear
When she did starve the general world beside
And prodigally gave them all to you.

GONERIL

Come, come, you talk greasily; your lips grow foul.

COSTARD

I do forswear them; and I here protest,
My love to thee is sound, sans crack or flaw.

GONERIL

Sans sans, I pray you.

EDMUND

Why, what a monstrous fellow art thou, thus to rail on one that is neither known of thee nor knows thee!

COSTARD

Fellow, I know thee.

EDMUND

What dost thou know me for?

COSTARD

A knave; a rascal; a base, proud, shallow, beggarly, three-suited, hundred-pound, filthy, worsted-stocking knave; a whoreson, glass-gazing, super-serviceable finical rogue; one-trunk-inheriting slave; one that wouldst be a bawd, in way of good service, and art nothing but the composition of a knave, beggar, coward, pandar, and the son and heir of a mongrel bitch—
But to return to the verses: did they please you, Princess Goneril?

GONERIL

O thou monster Ignorance, how deformed dost thou look!

*(Enter **KING LEAR**, **KENT** and Attendants.)*

KING LEAR

How now, daughter! what makes that frontlet on?
Methinks you are too much of late i' the frown.

GONERIL

Not only, sir, this your all-licensed fool,
But other of your insolent retinue
Do hourly carp and quarrel; breaking forth
In rank and not-to-be endurèd riots.
I have this present evening from my sister
Been well inform'd of them.

KING LEAR

                                    Are you our daughter?

GONERIL

    Here do you keep a hundred knights and squires;
Men so disorder'd, so debosh'd and bold,
The shame itself doth speak
For instant remedy: be then desired
A little to disquantity your train;
And the remainder, that shall still depend,
To be such men as may besort your age,
And know themselves and you.

KING LEAR

                                  Darkness and devils!
My train are men of choice and rarest parts,
That all particulars of duty know,
And in the most exact regard support
The worships of their name. O Lear, Lear, Lear!

    (Striking his head.)

Beat at this gate, that let thy folly in,
And thy dear judgment out! Go, go, my people.
[To **COSTARD***]* Suspend thy purpose, if thou didst intend
To make this creature fruitful!
Hear, nature, hear; dear goddess, hear!
Turn all her mother's pains and benefits
To laughter and contempt; that she may feel
How sharper than a serpent's tooth it is
To have a thankless child! Away, away!

COSTARD

    Shalt see thy other daughter will use thee kindly; for though she's as like this as a crab's like an apple, yet I can tell what I can tell.

KING LEAR

    Why, what canst thou tell, my boy?

COSTARD

    I can not tell.

KING LEAR

Go you before to Gloucester with these letters. Acquaint my daughter no further with any thing you know than comes from her demand out of the letter. If your diligence be not speedy, I shall be there afore you.

COSTARD

I will not sleep, my lord, till I have delivered your letter.

[To **GONERIL***]* Thou wast a pretty fellow when thou hadst no need to care for her frowning; now thou art an O without a figure: I am better than thou art now; I am a fool, thou art nothing.

   (*Exeunt* **COSTARD**, **KING LEAR** *and* **KENT**.)

EDMUND

The king is in high rage.

GONERIL

'Tis best to give him way; he leads himself.

   (*Enter* **OSWALD**.)

What, have you writ that letter to my sister?

OSWALD

Yes, madam.

GONERIL

[To **EDMUND***]* Thou, trusty servant
Shall pass between us: ere long you are like to hear,
If you dare venture in your own behalf,
A mistress's command. Wear this; spare speech;

   (*Giving him a favour.*)

Decline your head: this kiss, if it durst speak,
Would stretch thy spirits up into the air:
Conceive, and fare thee well.

EDMUND

Yours in the ranks of death.

GONERIL

                         My most dear Edmund!
Please you, draw near. Louder the music there!
O, the difference of man and man!

To thee a woman's services are due:
The fool usurps my body. Get you gone;
And hasten your return.
  (Exeunt.)

SCENE 5 - A garden.

(Enter **GLOUCESTER** *and* **JAQUENETTA**.*)*

GLOUCESTER
White-handed mistress, one sweet word with thee.
JAQUENETTA
Honey, and milk, and sugar; there is three.
GLOUCESTER
One word in secret.
JAQUENETTA
                    Let it not be sweet.
GLOUCESTER
Thou grievest my gall.
JAQUENETTA
                    Gall! bitter.
GLOUCESTER
                            Therefore meet.
I have promised to study three years with the king.
JAQUENETTA
You may do it in an hour, sir.
GLOUCESTER
Impossible.
JAQUENETTA
How many is one thrice told?
GLOUCESTER
It doth amount to one more than two.
JAQUENETTA
Now here is three studied, ere ye'll thrice wink: and how easy it is to put 'years' to the word 'three,' and study three years in two words, the dancing horse will tell you.
GLOUCESTER
A most fine figure!
JAQUENETTA
To prove you a cipher.

GLOUCESTER

Have you heard of no likely wars toward, 'twixt the Princess Regan and Goneril?

JAQUENETTA

Not a word.

GLOUCESTER

You may do, then, in time. Fare you well, sweet.

(Exeunt.)

SCENE 6 - Gloucester's castle.

(Enter **COSTARD** *and* **MUSICIANS**, *serenading beneath Regan's window.)*

COSTARD

[Sings] A woman, that is like a German clock,
Still a-repairing, ever out of frame,
And never going aright, being a watch,
But being watch'd that it may still go right!
And I to sigh for her! to watch for her!
To pray for her! Go to; it is a plague
That Cupid will impose for my neglect
Of his almighty dreadful little might.
What, I! I love! I sue! I seek a wife!
Well, I will love, write, sigh, pray, sue and groan:
Some men must love my lady and some Joan.

(Enter **REGAN**, **EDMUND** *and* **GLOUCESTER**.*)*

EDMUND

When were you wont to be so full of songs, sirrah?

REGAN

Was he not companion with the riotous knights
That tend upon my father?

GLOUCESTER

I know not, madam: 'tis too bad, too bad.

EDMUND

Yes, madam, he was of that consort.

REGAN

No marvel, then, though he were ill affected.

COSTARD

O, I am yours, and all that I possess!

REGAN

All the fool mine?

COSTARD

                    I cannot give you less.

REGAN

We have received your letters full of love;

Your favours, the ambassadors of love;
And, in our maiden council, rated them
In their own fashion, like a merriment.

COSTARD

Our letters, madam, show'd much more than jest.
So did our looks.

REGAN

                We did not quote them so.
[To **GLOUCESTER***]* I will not speak with him; say I am sick.

GLOUCESTER

[To **COSTARD***]* I am sorry for thee, friend; 'tis Regan's pleasure,
Whose disposition, all the world well knows,
Will not be rubb'd nor stopp'd.

COSTARD

Deny to speak with me? She is sick? she is weary? She has travell'd all the night?
Fetch me a better answer.

GLOUCESTER

                My dear fool,
You know the fiery quality of her grace;
How unremoveable and fix'd she is
In her own course.

COSTARD

Vengeance! plague! death! confusion!
Fiery? what quality?

EDMUND

Fetch forth the stocks! You stubborn braggart knave,
We'll teach you—

COSTARD

             Sir, I am too old to learn:
Call not your stocks for me: I serve the king:
You shall do small respect, show too bold malice
Against the grace and person of my master,
Stocking his messenger.

REGAN

Call them forth quickly; we will do so.

EDMUND

Fetch forth the stocks! As I have life and honour,
There shall he sit till noon.

REGAN

Till noon! till night, my lord; and all night too.

COSTARD

Why, madam, if I were your father's dog,
You should not use me so.

EDMUND

       Sir, being his knave, I will.

REGAN

This is a fellow of the self-same colour
Our sister speaks of. Come, bring away the stocks!

(Stocks brought out.)

GLOUCESTER

Let me beseech your grace not to do so:
His fault is much, and the good king his master
Will cheque him for 't: your purposed low correction
Is such as basest and contemned'st wretches
Are punish'd with: the king must take it ill,
That he's so slightly valued in his messenger,
Should have him thus restrain'd.

REGAN

       Put in his legs.

*(**COSTARD** is put in the stocks.)*

Come, my good lord, away.

*(Exeunt all but **COSTARD**.)*

COSTARD

That sir which serves and seeks for gain,
And follows but for form,
Will pack when it begins to rain,
And leave thee in the storm,
But I will tarry; the fool will stay,
And let the wise man fly:
The knave turns fool that runs away;
The fool no knave, perdy.

*(Enter **KING LEAR** and **KENT**.)*

KING LEAR
'Tis strange that she should so depart from home,
And not send back my messenger.

COSTARD
Hail to thee, noble master!

KING LEAR
Ha!
What's he that hath so much thy place mistook
To set thee here?

COSTARD
      It is not he, but she;
Your daughter Regan.

KING LEAR
        No.

COSTARD
         Yes.

KING LEAR
         No, I say.

COSTARD
I say, yea.

KING LEAR
    No, no, she would not.

COSTARD
          Yes, she has.

KING LEAR
By Jupiter, I swear, no.

COSTARD
By Juno, I swear, ay.

KING LEAR
       She durst not do 't;
She could not, would not do 't; 'tis worse than murder,
To do upon respect such violent outrage:
Resolve me, with all modest haste, which way
Thou mightst deserve, or they impose, this usage.
An you lie, sirrah, we'll have you whipped.

COSTARD

I marvel what kin thou and thy daughters are: they'll have me whipped for speaking true, thou'lt have me whipped for lying; and sometimes I am whipped for holding my peace.

(Enter **GLOUCESTER**.*)*

KING LEAR

Why, Gloucester, Gloucester,
I'ld speak with the Princess Regan, call her forth.

GLOUCESTER

Well, my good lord, I have inform'd her so.

KING LEAR

Inform'd her! Dost thou understand me, man?
The king would speak with Regan; the dear father
Would with his daughter speak, commands her service:
Is she inform'd of this? My breath and blood!
Go tell her ladyship I'ld speak with her,
Now, presently: bid her come forth and hear me.

GLOUCESTER

I would have all well betwixt you.

(Exit.)

KING LEAR

O me, my heart, my rising heart! but, down!

(Enter **REGAN**, **EDMUND**, **GLOUCESTER**, *and Servants.)*

EDMUND

Hail to your grace!

*(***COSTARD** *is set at liberty.)*

REGAN

I am glad to see your highness.

KING LEAR

Some other time for that. Belovèd Regan,
Thy sister's naught: O Regan, she hath tied
Sharp-tooth'd unkindness, like a vulture, here:

(Points to his heart.)

I can scarce speak to thee; thou'lt not believe
With how depraved a quality—O Regan!

REGAN

    I cannot think my sister in the least
    Would fail her obligation: if, sir, perchance
    She have restrain'd the riots of your followers,
    'Tis on such ground, and to such wholesome end,
    As clears her from all blame.

KING LEAR

    My curses on her!

REGAN

                      O, sir, you are old.

KING LEAR

    All the stored vengeances of heaven fall
    On her ingrateful top! Strike her young bones!

REGAN

    O the blest gods! so will you wish on me,
    When the rash mood is on.

KING LEAR

    No, Regan, thou shalt never have my curse:
    Thy half o' the kingdom hast thou not forgot,
    Wherein I thee endow'd.

REGAN

                      Good sir, to the purpose.

KING LEAR

    Who stock'd my servant? Regan, I have good hope
    Thou didst not know on't.

    (Tucket within.)

                      Who comes here? O heavens,

    (Enter **GONERIL***.)*

    If you do love old men, if your sweet sway
    Allow obedience, if yourselves are old,
    Make it your cause; send down, and take my part!
    [To **GONERIL***]* Art not ashamed to look upon this beard?
    O Regan, wilt thou take her by the hand?

GONERIL

    Why not by the hand, sir? How have I offended?

All's not offence that indiscretion finds
And dotage terms so.
KING LEAR
                              O sides, you are too tough;
Will you yet hold? How came my man i' the stocks?
REGAN
I set him there, sir: but his own disorders
Deserved much less advancement.
KING LEAR
                                            You! did you?
REGAN
I pray you, father, being weak, seem so.
If, till the expiration of your month,
You will return and sojourn with my sister,
Dismissing half your train, come then to me:
I am now from home, and out of that provision
Which shall be needful for your entertainment.
KING LEAR
Return to her, and fifty men dismiss'd?
No, rather I abjure all roofs, and choose
To wage against the enmity o' the air.
GONERIL
At your choice, sir.
KING LEAR
I prithee, daughter, do not make me mad:
I can be patient; I can stay with Regan,
I and my hundred knights.
REGAN
                                 Not altogether so:
I look'd not for you yet, nor am provided
For your fit welcome. If you will come to me,
Sir, bring but five and twenty: to no more
Will I give place or notice.
KING LEAR
I gave you all—
REGAN
                            And in good time you gave it.

KING LEAR

But five and twenty, Regan? said you so?

REGAN

And speak't again, my lord; no more with me.

KING LEAR

[To **GONERIL***]* I'll go with thee:
Thy fifty yet doth double five and twenty,
And thou art twice her love.

GONERIL

                                Hear me, my lord;
What need you five and twenty, ten, or five,
To follow in a house where twice so many
Have a command to tend you?

REGAN

                                          What need one?

KING LEAR

You heavens, give me that patience, patience I need!
I will have such revenges on you both,
What they are, yet I know not: but they shall be
The terrors of the earth. You think I'll weep
No, I'll not weep:

(Storm and tempest.)

I have full cause of weeping; but this heart
Shall break into a hundred thousand flaws,
Or ere I'll weep. O fool, I shall go mad!

(Exeunt **KING LEAR** *and* **KENT**, *escorted by* **GLOUCESTER** *and* **EDMUND**.*)*

COSTARD

Thou changèd and self-cover'd things, for shame:
Proper deformity seems not in the fiend
So horrid as in woman.

REGAN

                                    O vain fool!

COSTARD

You are not worth the dust which the rude wind
Blows in your face.

GONERIL

Marry, your manhood now—

(Exit **COSTARD**.*)*

REGAN

Are these the breed of wits so wonder'd at?

GONERIL

Well, better wits have worn plain statute-caps.
But will you hear? the swain is my love sworn.

REGAN

The coxcomb here hath plighted faith to me.

GONERIL

And swore that he was for my service born.

REGAN

The fool is mine, as sure as bark on tree.

GONERIL

We are wise girls to mock our lover so.

REGAN

He the worse fool to purchase mocking so.

GONERIL

Let us withdraw; 'twill be a storm.

(Re-enter **GLOUCESTER** *and* **EDMUND**.*)*

GLOUCESTER

Alack, the night comes on, and the bleak winds
Do sorely ruffle; for many miles a bout
There's scarce a bush.

REGAN

                O, sir, to wilful men,
The injuries that they themselves procure
Must be their schoolmasters. Shut up your doors:
He is attended with a desperate train.

GONERIL

Shut up your doors, my lord; 'tis a wild night:
My Regan counsels well; come out o' the storm.

(Exeunt **GLOUCESTER** *and* **GONERIL**.*)*

REGAN

Shall I hear from you anon?

EDMUND

I do serve you in this business.

REGAN

Play, music, then! Nay, you must do it soon.

   (Musicians play.)

The music plays; vouchsafe some motion to it.

EDMUND

Our ears vouchsafe it.

REGAN

                              But your legs should do it.

EDMUND

If you desire to dance, let's hold more chat.

REGAN

In private, then.

EDMUND

                      I am best pleased with that.

   (Exeunt.)

End of Act III

ACT IV - Madness & Blindness

SCENE 1 - A heath.

(Storm still. Enter **KENT** *and* **JAQUENETTA**.*)*

JAQUENETTA
Who's there, besides foul weather?
KENT
One minded like the weather, most unquietly.
JAQUENETTA
I know you. Where's the king?
KENT
Contending with the fretful element.
JAQUENETTA
But who is with him?
KENT
None but the fool; who labours to out-jest
His heart-struck injuries.
JAQUENETTA
                    Sir, I do know you;
And dare, upon the warrant of my note,
Commend a dear thing to you. There is division,
Although as yet the face of it be cover'd
With mutual cunning, 'twixt Goneril and Regan;
Who have—look you—servants, who seem no less,
Which are to France the spies and speculations
Intelligent of our state.
KENT
And true it is, from France there comes a power
Into this scatter'd kingdom; who already,
Wise in our negligence, have secret feet
In some of our best ports, and are at point
To show their open banner. Now to you:

(Gives her a letter.)

If on my credit Gloucester dare so far
To make his speed to Dover, he shall find
Some that will thank him, making just report
Of how unnatural and bemadding sorrow
The king hath cause to plain.

JAQUENETTA

I will talk further with you.

KENT

                                        No, do not.
I will go seek the king. Fie on this storm!

(Exeunt severally.)

SCENE 2 - Another part of the heath.

*(Storm still. Enter **KING LEAR** and **COSTARD**.)*

KING LEAR

Blow, winds, and crack your cheeks! rage! blow!
You cataracts and hurricanoes, spout
Till you have drench'd our steeples, drown'd the cocks!
You sulphurous and thought-executing fires,
Singe my white head! And thou, all-shaking thunder,
Smite flat the thick rotundity o' the world!
By the Lord, this love is as mad as Ajax: it kills sheep; it kills me, I a sheep: well proved again o' my side! I will not love: if I do, hang me; i' faith, I will not.

COSTARD

Good nuncle, in, and ask thy daughters' blessing: here's a night pities neither wise man nor fool.

KING LEAR

Rumble thy bellyful! Spit, fire! spout, rain!
Nor rain, wind, thunder, fire, are my daughters:
But yet I call you servile ministers,
That have with two pernicious daughters join'd
Your high engender'd battles 'gainst a head
So old and white as this. O! O! 'tis foul!

COSTARD

He that has a house to put's head in has a good head-piece.

KING LEAR

Comfort me, boy: what great men have been in love?

COSTARD

Hercules, master.

KING LEAR

Most sweet Hercules! More authority, dear boy, name more; and, sweet my child, let them be men of good repute and carriage.

COSTARD

Samson, master: he was a man of good carriage, great carriage, for he carried the town-gates on his back like a porter: and he was in love.

KING LEAR

O well-knit Samson! strong-jointed Samson! I do excel thee in my rapier as much as thou didst me in carrying gates. I am in love too.
I would forget her; but a fever she
Reigns in my blood and will remember'd be.

(Enter **KENT**.*)*

KENT

Alas, sir, are you here? things that love night
Love not such nights as these. Alack, bare-headed!

KING LEAR

[To **KENT***]* Go, tenderness of years; take this key, give enlargement to the swain, bring him festinately hither: I must employ him in a letter to my love.

COSTARD

A message well sympathized; a horse to be ambassador for an ass.

KING LEAR

[To **COSTARD***]* O, are you free? My wits begin to turn.
O, let me not be mad, not mad, sweet heaven
Keep me in temper: I would not be mad!

KENT

Sir, do you know me?

KING LEAR

Dost thou know me, fellow?

COSTARD

My boon I make it, that you know me not.

KING LEAR

Fetch hither the swain: he must carry me a letter.

(Exeunt.)

SCENE 3 - Gloucester's castle.

(Enter **GLOUCESTER** *and* **EDMUND**.*)*

GLOUCESTER

Alack, alack, Edmund, I like not this unnatural dealing. When I desire their leave that I might pity him, they took from me the use of mine own house; charged me, on pain of their perpetual displeasure, neither to speak of him, entreat for him, nor any way sustain him.

EDMUND

Most savage and unnatural!

GLOUCESTER

Go to; say you nothing. There's a division betwixt the sisters; and a worse matter than that: I have received a letter this night; 'tis dangerous to be spoken; I have locked the letter in my closet: these injuries the king now bears will be revenged home: I will seek him, and privily relieve him: go you and maintain talk with the princesses: if they ask for me. I am ill, and gone to bed. Though I die for it, the king my old master must be relieved.

(Exit.)

EDMUND

This courtesy, forbid thee, shall the sisters
Instantly know; and of that letter too:
This seems a fair deserving, and must draw me
That which my father loses; no less than all:
The younger rises when the old doth fall.

(Exit.)

SCENE 4 - The French camp, near Dover.

(Enter the **PRINCESS**, **CORDELIA** *and* **BOYET**.*)*

PRINCESS
Sweet heart, we shall be rich ere we return:
Look you what I have from the loving king.

CORDELIA
Madame, came nothing else along with that?

PRINCESS
Nothing but this! yes, as much love in rhyme
As would be cramm'd up in a sheet of paper.
But, lady, here you have a favour too:
Who sent it? and what is it?

CORDELIA
                              I would you knew:
Nay, I have verses too, I thank Lord Kent:
The numbers true; and, were the numbering too,
I were the fairest goddess on the ground:
I am compared to twenty thousand fairs.
O, he hath drawn my picture in his letter!

BOYET
Any thing like?

CORDELIA
Much in the letters; nothing in the praise.

BOYET
Beauteous as ink; a good conclusion.

PRINCESS
Will you hear this letter with attention?

CORDELIA
As we would hear an oracle.

PRINCESS
[Reads] 'By heaven, that thou art fair, is most infallible; true, that thou art beauteous; truth itself, that thou art lovely. More fairer than fair, beautiful than beauteous, truer than truth itself, have commiseration on thy heroical vassal!—'

(As she reads...)

SCENE 5 - The heath. Before a hovel.

*(Enter **KING LEAR** upon the stormy heath, dictating the same to **COSTARD**, with pen and paper, following.)*

KING LEAR

Yet was Samson so tempted, and he had an excellent strength; yet was Solomon so seduced, and he had a very good wit. Cupid's butt-shaft is too hard for Hercules' club; and therefore too much odds for a Spaniard's rapier; the passado he respects not, the duello he regards not: his disgrace is to be called boy; but his glory is to subdue men. Adieu, valour! rust rapier! be still, drum! for your manager is in love; yea, he loveth.

COSTARD

This cold night will turn us all to fools and madmen.

KING LEAR

'Tis true indeed. Sing, boy; my spirit grows heavy in love.

COSTARD

And that's great marvel, loving a light wench.

KING LEAR

I say, sing.

COSTARD

[Singing] He that has and a little tiny wit—
With hey, ho, the wind and the rain,—
Must make content with his fortunes fit,
For the rain it raineth every day.

*(Enter **KENT**.)*

KENT

Gracious my lord, hard by here is a hovel;
Some friendship will it lend you 'gainst the tempest.

(Storm still.)

KING LEAR

*[To **COSTARD**]* In, boy; go first. You houseless poverty,—
Nay, get thee in. I'll pray, and then I'll sleep.

*(**COSTARD** goes in.)*

EDGAR

[Within] Fathom and half, fathom and half! Poor Tom!

(**COSTARD** *runs out from the hovel.*)

COSTARD

Come not in here, nuncle, here's a spirit. Help me, help me!

KENT

Give me thy hand. Who's there?

(*Enter* **EDGAR**, *disguised as a mad man.*)

EDGAR

Away! the foul fiend follows me! Through the sharp hawthorn blows the cold wind. Hum! go to thy cold bed, and warm thee.

KING LEAR

Hast thou given all to thy two daughters? And art thou come to this?

EDGAR

Who gives any thing to poor Tom? whom the foul fiend hath led through fire and through flame, and through ford and whirlipool e'er bog and quagmire; that hath laid knives under his pillow, and halters in his pew; set ratsbane by his porridge; made film proud of heart, to ride on a bay trotting-horse over four-inched bridges, to course his own shadow for a traitor. Bless thy five wits! Tom's a-cold,—O, do de, do de, do de.

(*Storm still.*)

KING LEAR

What, have his daughters brought him to this pass?

KENT

He hath no daughters, sir.

KING LEAR

Death, traitor! nothing could have subdued nature
To such a lowness but his unkind daughters.
He's mad that trusts in the tameness of a wolf, a horse's health, a daughter's love, or a lady's oath.

EDGAR

The foul fiend haunts poor Tom in the voice of a nightingale. Hopdance cries in Tom's belly for two white herring. Croak not, black angel; I have no food for thee.

KING LEAR

Is it the fashion, that discarded fathers
Should have thus little mercy on their flesh?
Couldst thou save nothing? Didst thou give them all?

COSTARD

Nay, he reserved a blanket, else we had been all shamed.

KING LEAR

Judicious punishment! 'twas this flesh begot
Those pelican daughters.

EDGAR

Pillicock sat on Pillicock-hill: Halloo, halloo, loo, loo! Take heed o' the foul fiend. Tom's a-cold.

(Storm still.)

KING LEAR

Why, thou wert better in thy grave than to answer with thy uncovered body this extremity of the skies. Is man no more than this? Consider him well. Thou art the thing itself: unaccommodated man is no more but such a poor bare, forked animal as thou art. Off, off, you lendings! come unbutton here.

(Tearing off his clothes.)

Pull off my boots: harder, harder: so.

COSTARD

Prithee, nuncle, be contented; 'tis a naughty night to swim in.

EDGAR

Look, here comes a walking fire.

*(Enter **GLOUCESTER** and **JAQUENETTA**, with a torch.)*

This is the foul fiend Flibbertigibbet: aroint thee, witch, aroint thee!

KENT

Who's there? What is't you seek?

GLOUCESTER

What are you there? Your names?

EDGAR

Poor Tom; that eats the swimming frog, the toad, the tadpole, the wall-newt and the water. Beware my follower. Peace, Smulkin; peace, thou fiend!

JAQUENETTA

What, hath your grace no better company?

EDGAR

The prince of darkness is a gentleman: Modo he's call'd, and Mahu.

GLOUCESTER

Go in with me: my duty cannot suffer
To obey in all your daughters' hard commands:
Though their injunction be to bar my doors,
And let this tyrannous night take hold upon you.

COSTARD

Good my lord, take his offer; go into the house.

KENT

Importune him once more to go, my lord;
His wits begin to unsettle.

GLOUCESTER

                        Canst thou blame him?

(Storm still.)

His daughters seek his death:
Thou say'st the king grows mad; I'll tell thee, friend,
I am almost mad myself: I had a son,
Now outlaw'd from my blood; he sought my wife,
But lately, very late: I loved him, friend;
No father his son dearer: truth to tell thee,
The grief hath crazed my wits. What a night's this!

EDGAR

Tom's a-cold.

GLOUCESTER

In, fellow, there, into the hovel: keep thee warm.

KING LEAR

I will keep still with my philosopher.

KENT

Good my lord, soothe him; let him take the fellow.

KING LEAR

Come, good Athenian.

GLOUCESTER

      No words, no words: hush.

(Exeunt **KING LEAR**, **EDGAR** *and* **COSTARD**, *into the hovel.)*

KENT

All the power of his wits have given way to his impatience: the gods reward your kindness!

GLOUCESTER

Here is better than the open air. I will piece out the comfort with what addition I can: I will not be long from you.

(Exeunt.)

SCENE 6 - Gloucester's castle.

(Enter **REGAN** *and* **EDMUND**.*)*

REGAN

I will have my revenge ere I depart his house.

EDMUND

This is the letter he spoke of, which approves him an intelligent party to the advantages of France: O heavens! that this treason were not, or not I the detector!

REGAN

True or false, it hath made thee Earl of Gloucester. Seek out where thy father is, that he may be ready for our apprehension.

EDMUND

[Aside] If I find him comforting the king, it will stuff his suspicion more fully.

REGAN

I will lay trust upon thee; and thou shalt find a dearer fortune in my love.

(Enter **GONERIL**, *and Servants.)*

GONERIL

How now! where's the king?

EDMUND

My father Gloucester hath convey'd him hence:
Some five or six and thirty of his knights
Are gone with him towards Dover; where they boast
To have well-armèd friends.

GONERIL

Post speedily to our powers; show them this letter: the army of France is landed. Seek out the villain Gloucester.

(Exeunt some of the Servants.)

REGAN

Hang him instantly.

GONERIL

Pluck out his eyes.

REGAN

Leave him to our displeasure. Edmund: the revenges we are bound to take upon your traitorous father are not fit for your beholding.

GONERIL

Get horses for his lordship.

REGAN

Farewell, dear Edmund: farewell, my lord of Gloucester.

GONERIL

Edmund, farewell.

(Exit **EDMUND***.)*

REGAN

Go seek the traitor Gloucester,
Pinion him like a thief, bring him before us.

(Exeunt other Servants.)

GLOUCESTER

[Within] What mean'st by this?

REGAN

Who's there? the traitor?

(Enter **GLOUCESTER***, brought in by two or three.)*

GONERIL

Ingrateful fox! 'tis he.

REGAN

Bind fast his corky arms.

GLOUCESTER

What mean your graces? Good my friends, consider
You are my guests: do me no foul play, friends.

GONERIL

Come, sir, what letters had you late from France?

REGAN

Be simple answerer, for we know the truth.

GONERIL

And what confederacy have you with the traitors
Late footed in the kingdom?

REGAN

To whose hands have you sent the lunatic king? Speak.

GLOUCESTER

I have a letter guessingly set down,
Which came from one that's of a neutral heart,
And not from one opposed.

GONERIL

Cunning.

REGAN

And false.

(**REGAN** *plucks his beard.*)

GLOUCESTER

By the kind gods, 'tis most ignobly done
To pluck me by the beard. I am your host:
With robbers' hands my hospitable favours
You should not ruffle thus. What will you do?

REGAN

Though well we may not pass upon your life
Without the form of justice, yet our power
Shall do a courtesy to our wrath, which men
May blame, but not control.

GONERIL

Bring in the evidence.

JAQUENETTA

[Within] Help, ho! murder! murder!

(**JAQUENETTA** *brought in.*)

REGAN

To this chair bind her.

(*Servants bind* **JAQUENETTA**.)

GLOUCESTER

What mean you, madam?

(*A Servant brings* **GONERIL** *a copy of the king's proclamation of vows.*)

GONERIL

[Reads] 'Item, That no man shall be seen to talk with a woman within the term of three years—'

REGAN

Hath this been proclaimed?

GONERIL

Four days ago.

REGAN

Let's see the penalty.

GONERIL

[Reads] 'On pain of losing her tongue.'

REGAN

Who devised this penalty?

GLOUCESTER

Marry, that did I.

REGAN

Sweet lord, and why?

GLOUCESTER

To fright them hence with that dread penalty.

GONERIL

A dangerous law against gentility!

REGAN

[To **JAQUENETTA***]* Spake you with him?

GONERIL

She cannot deny it.

JAQUENETTA

I am tied to the stake, and I must stand the course.

REGAN

Where hast thou sent the king?

JAQUENETTA

To Dover.

GONERIL

Wherefore to Dover? Wast thou not charged at peril—

REGAN

Wherefore to Dover? Let her first answer that.

GONERIL

Wherefore to Dover, maid?

JAQUENETTA

Because we would not see thy cruel nails
Pluck out his poor old eyes; nor thy fierce sister
In his anointed flesh stick boarish fangs.
All cruels else subscribed: but I shall see
The wingèd vengeance overtake such children.

GONERIL

See't shalt thou never. Fellows, hold the chair.
Upon these eyes of thine I'll set my foot.

JAQUENETTA

He that will think to live till he be old,
Give me some help!

>   (**GONERIL** *gouges out* **JAQUENETTA**'s *eye.*)

                    O cruel! O you gods!

REGAN

One side will mock another; the other too.

GONERIL

If you see vengeance,—

GLOUCESTER

                    Hold your hand, my lady:
I have served you ever since you were a child;
But better service have I never done you
Than now to bid you hold.

REGAN

                      How now, you dog!

GLOUCESTER

If you did wear a beard upon your chin,
I'd shake it on this quarrel. What do you mean?

GONERIL

My villain!

>   (*They draw and fight.*)

GLOUCESTER

Nay, then, come on, and take the chance of anger.

LEAR'S LABOUR'S LOST

REGAN
Give me thy sword. A vassal stand up thus!
(Takes a sword, and runs at him behind.)

GLOUCESTER
O, I am slain! My sweet, you have one eye left
To see some mischief on them. O!

GONERIL
Lest it see more, prevent it. Out, vile jelly!
(Gouges out her other eye.)
Where is thy lustre now?

JAQUENETTA
All dark and comfortless.

GLOUCESTER
Where's my son Edmund?
Edmund, enkindle all the sparks of nature,
To quit this horrid act.

REGAN
Out, treacherous villain!
Thou call'st on him that hates thee: it was he
That made the overture of thy treasons to us;
Who is too good to pity thee.

GLOUCESTER
O my follies! then Edgar was abused.
Kind gods, forgive me that, and prosper him!
(Dies.)

REGAN
What, is he dead?

GONERIL
Turn out that eyeless villain; throw this slave
Upon the dunghill.

REGAN
Go thrust her out at gates, and let her smell
Her way to Dover.
*(Exeunt **GONERIL** and **REGAN**.)*

FIRST SERVANT
>I'll never care what wickedness I do,
>If these two come to good.

SECOND SERVANT
>   If they live long,
>And in the end meet the old course of death,
>Women will all turn monsters.

>*(Exeunt.)*

SCENE 7 - The French camp, near Dover.

(Enter **CORDELIA** *and* **KENT**.*)*

CORDELIA
What news?
KENT
O, majesty, the Duke of Gloucester's dead:
Slain by your sister, going to put out
The other eye of Gloucester's serving maid.
Opposed against the act, bending his sword
Against the princess; who, thereat enraged,
Flew on him, and amongst them fell'd him dead.
CORDELIA
But, O poor Jaquenetta!
Lost she her other eye?
KENT
                              Both, both, my lady.
CORDELIA
Where was his son when they did take her eyes?
KENT
He was not there.
CORDELIA
                    Knows he the wickedness?
KENT
Ay, majesty; 'twas he inform'd against them;
And quit the house on purpose, that their punishment
Might have the freer course.
CORDELIA
                              Gloucester, I live
To thank thee for the love thou show'dst the king,
And to revenge thy Jaquenetta's eyes.
Come hither, friend: Tell me what more thou know'st.

(Exeunt.)

SCENE 8 - Gloucester's castle.

(Enter **GONERIL** *and* **OSWALD**, *with a letter.)*

GONERIL
From Regan, Edmund's mistress salutations?
OSWALD
Yes, madam.
GONERIL
Why should she write to Edmund? Might not you
Transport her purposes by word? Belike,
Something—I know not what: I'll love thee much,
Let me unseal the letter.
OSWALD
                            Madam, I had rather—
GONERIL
Lord Edmund spake not with her grace at home?
OSWALD
No, madam.
GONERIL
What might import my sister's letter to him?
OSWALD
I know not, lady.
GONERIL
I know your lady does not love her Edgar;
I am sure of that: at her late being here
She gave strange oeillades and most speaking looks
To noble Edmund. I know you are of her bosom.
OSWALD
I, madam?
GONERIL
I speak in understanding; you are; I know't:
I pray, desire her call her wisdom to her:
Her lord is fled; Edmund and I have talk'd;
And more convenient is he for my hand
Than for your lady's:—
OSWALD
I must needs after him, madam, with my letter—

*(**GONERIL** draws a sword and stabs him in the back.)*

GONERIL

So, fare you well.

OSWALD

Wench, thou hast slain me: O, untimely death!

*(Dies. **GONERIL** opens his letters.)*

GONERIL

Leave, gentle wax; and, manners, blame us not:
To know our enemies' minds, we'ld rip their hearts;
Their papers, is more lawful.
[Reads] 'Let our reciprocal vows be remembered. You may have opportunities to cut him off: if your will want not, time and place will be fruitfully offered. There is nothing done, if he return: then am I the prisoner, and his bed my goal; from the loathed warmth whereof deliver me, and supply the place for your labour.
Your affectionate servant, REGAN.'
A plot upon the virtuous Edgar's life;
And in exchange his brother! For him 'tis well
That of thy death and business I can tell.

(Exit.)

SCENE 9 - Gloucester's castle.

(Enter **EDMUND** *and* **REGAN**.*)*

REGAN

Our sister's man is certainly miscarried.

EDMUND

'Tis to be doubted, madam.

REGAN

Now, sweet lord,
You know the goodness I intend upon you:
Tell me—but truly—but then speak the truth,
Do you not love my sister?

EDMUND

In honour'd love.

REGAN

But have you never found a lover's way
To the forfended place?

EDMUND

That thought abuses you.

REGAN

I am doubtful that you have been conjunct
And bosom'd with her, as far as we call hers.

EDMUND

No, by mine honour, madam.

REGAN

I never shall endure her: dear my lord,
Be not familiar with her.

EDMUND

Fear me not.
I will visit thee at the lodge.

REGAN

[Aside] I had rather lose the battle than that sister
Should loosen him and me.

(Exit.)

EDMUND

To both these sisters have I sworn my love;

Each jealous of the other, as the stung
Are of the adder. Which of them shall I take?
Both? one? or neither? Neither can be enjoy'd,
If both remain alive: to take the younger
Exasperates, makes mad her sister Goneril;
And hardly shall I carry out my side,
My brother being alive. Therefore my state
Stands on me to defend, not to debate.
Let her who would be rid of him devise
His speedy taking off.
   (Exit.)

SCENE 10 - The heath.

(Enter **EDGAR** *with a challenge letter.)*

EDGAR

How light and portable my pain seems now,
When that which makes me bend makes the king bow,
He childed as I father'd! Tom, away!
Mark the high noises; and thyself bewray,
When false opinion, whose wrong thought defiles thee,
In thy just proof, repeals and reconciles thee.
What will hap more to-night, safe 'scape the king!
But who comes here?

(Enter **JAQUENETTA**, *led by a Servant.)*

My father's serving maid? World, world, O world!

JAQUENETTA

No farther, sir; a maid may rot even here.
Away, get thee away; good friend, be gone.

SERVANT

Alack, maid, you cannot see your way.

JAQUENETTA

I have no way, and therefore want no eyes.
Now, fellow, fare thee well: let go my hand;
Go farther off: I shall no leading need.

(Exit Servant.)

With all my heart, if Edgar live, O, bless him!
Might I but live to see thee in my touch,
I'ld say I had eyes again!

EDGAR

[Aside] O gods! Who is't can say 'I am at the worst'?
I am worse than e'er I was.

JAQUENETTA

O you mighty gods!
This world I do renounce, and, in your sights,
Shake patiently my great affliction off—

(Collapses.)

EDGAR

> Thus might she pass indeed: yet she revives.
> Hear you, girl! Speak!

JAQUENETTA

> > Away, and let me die.
> Is wretchedness deprived that benefit,
> To end itself by death?

EDGAR

> > But thou dost breathe;
> Do but look up.

JAQUENETTA

> > Alack, I have no eyes.
> Is that the naked fellow?

EDGAR

> > Ay, my lady.
> 'Tis poor mad Tom.

JAQUENETTA

> Methinks thy voice is alter'd; and thou speak'st
> In better phrase and matter than thou didst.

EDGAR

> You're much deceived: in nothing am I changed.

JAQUENETTA

> Methinks you're better spoken.
>
> *(Touches his face.)*
>
> O master Edgar,
> The food of thy abusèd father's wrath!
> Thy life's a miracle. Speak yet again.

EDGAR

> Give me your arm:
> Up: so. How is 't? Feel you your legs? You stand.

JAQUENETTA

> Too well, too well.

EDGAR

> Think that the clearest gods, who make them honours
> Of men's impossibilities, have preserved thee.

JAQUENETTA
> You ever-gentle gods, henceforth I'll bear
> Affliction till it do cry out itself.
> Let not my worser spirit tempt me again
> To die before you please!

EDGAR
>   But who comes here?

*(Enter **KING LEAR**, fantastically dressed with wild flowers.)*

KING LEAR
> No, they cannot touch me for coining; I am the king himself.

EDGAR
> O thou side-piercing sight!

JAQUENETTA
> I know that voice.

KING LEAR
> Ha! They flattered me like a dog; and told me I had white hairs in my beard ere the black ones were there.

JAQUENETTA
> Is 't not the king?

KING LEAR
>   Ay, every inch a king:
> When I do stare, see how the subject quakes.
> I pardon that man's life. What was thy cause? Adultery?
> Thou shalt not die: die for adultery! No:
> Let copulation thrive; for Gloucester's bastard son
> Was kinder to his father than my daughters
> Got 'tween the lawful sheets.

JAQUENETTA
> O ruin'd piece of nature! This great world
> Shall so wear out to nought. Dost thou know me?

KING LEAR
> I remember thine eyes well enough. Dost thou squiny at me?
> I know thee well enough; thy name is Gloucester.

JAQUENETTA
> Alack, alack the day!

KING LEAR

I'll be sworn, he wore none but a dishclout of Jaquenetta's, and that a' wears next his heart for a favour.

(Enter **BOYET**, *with Attendants.)*

BOYET

O, here he is: lay hand upon him. Sir,
Your most dear daughter—

KING LEAR

No rescue? What, a prisoner? Use me well;
You shall have ransom. Let me have surgeons;
I am cut to the brains.

BOYET

You shall have any thing.

KING LEAR

Then there's life in't. Nay, if you get it, you shall get it with running. Sa, sa, sa, sa.

(Exit running. Attendants follow.)

EDGAR

When we our betters see bearing our woes,
We scarcely think our miseries our foes.

BOYET

A sight most pitiful in the meanest wretch,
Past speaking of in a king! Thou hast one daughter,
Who redeems nature from the general curse
Which twain have brought her to.

(Enter, with drum and colours, **CORDELIA**, **PRINCESS**, **KENT**, *and Soldiers.)*

CORDELIA

Alack, 'tis he: why, he was met even now
As mad as the vex'd sea; singing aloud;
Crown'd with rank fumiter and furrow-weeds.

PRINCESS

Search every acre in the high-grown field,
And bring him to our eye.

(Exit an Officer.)

CORDELIA

                                    What can man's wisdom
In the restoring his bereavèd sense?

BOYET

There is means, madam:
Our foster-nurse of nature is repose,
The which he lacks; that to provoke in him,
Are many simples operative, whose power
Will close the eye of anguish.

CORDELIA

                                          All blest secrets,
All you unpublish'd virtues of the earth,
Spring with my tears! be aidant and remediate
In the good man's distress! Seek, seek for him;
Lest his ungovern'd rage dissolve the life
That wants the means to lead it.

EDGAR

[To **PRINCESS***]* If e'er your grace had speech with man so poor,
Hear me one word.

PRINCESS

                            I'll overtake you. Speak.

(Exeunt all but **PRINCESS** *and* **EDGAR**.*)*

EDGAR

Before you fight the battle, ope this letter.
If you have victory, let the trumpet sound
And I'll appear again; wretch though I seem,
I can produce a champion that will prove
What is avouchèd there.

PRINCESS

Stay till I have read the letter.

EDGAR

                                  I was forbid it.
When time shall serve, let but the herald cry.

PRINCESS

Why, fare thee well: I will o'erlook thy paper.

(Exeunt.)

End of Act IV

ACT V - Revenge & Revolution

SCENE 1 - The sisters' camp, near Dover.

(Enter **EDMUND** *and* **REGAN**.*)*

EDMUND

The enemy's in view; draw up your powers.
Here is the guess of their true strength and forces
By diligent discovery; but your haste
Is now urged on you.

REGAN

      We will greet the time.

EDMUND

Know of the princess if her purpose hold,
Or whether since she is advised by aught
To change the course: she's full of alteration
And self-reproving: bring her constant pleasure.

(Enter, with drum and colours, **GONERIL**, *and Soldiers.)*

REGAN

Our very loving sister, well be-met.

GONERIL

[To **EDMUND***]* Sir, this I hear; the king is come to his daughter,
With others whom the rigor of our state
Forced to cry out. Where I could not be honest,
I never yet was valiant: for this business,
It toucheth us, as France invades our land;
For these domestic and particular broils
Are not the question here.

REGAN

      Let's then determine
With the ancient of war on our proceedings.

EDMUND

I shall attend you presently at your tent.

REGAN

Sister, you'll go with us?

GONERIL

No.

REGAN

'Tis most convenient; pray you, go with us.

GONERIL

[Aside] O, ho, I know the riddle.—I will go.

(Exeunt **GONERIL** *and* **REGAN**.*)*

EDMUND

Come hither, herald. Where's thy drum?

HERALD

That's hereby.

EDMUND

Good friend, I prithee, take thy drum in arms;
There is a litter ready; lay that in 't,
And drive towards Dover, friend, where thou shalt beat,
From morn till night, upon the crown o' the cliff.

HERALD

Well, I will do it, sir: fare you well.

(Exit.)

EDMUND

It were a delicate stratagem, to shoe
A troop of horse with felt: I'll put 't in proof;
And when I have stol'n upon these enemies,
Then, kill, kill, kill, kill, kill, kill!

(Exit.)

SCENE 2 - A tent in the French camp.

*(**LEAR** on a bed asleep; **BOYET**, and others attending; Enter the **PRINCESS** and **CORDELIA**, with **KENT**, disguised as a Soldier of Navarre.)*

CORDELIA
Why are you here but even now disguised?
KENT
Yet to be known shortens my made intent.
CORDELIA
But in this changing what is your intent?
KENT
The effect of my intent is to cross theirs.
PRINCESS
Of Goneril's and Regan's powers you heard ought?
KENT
'Tis so, they are afoot.
PRINCESS
'Tis time to look about; the powers of the kingdom approach apace.
CORDELIA
The arbitrement is like to be bloody. Fare you well, sir.
KENT
Proud of employment, willingly I go.
CORDELIA
All pride is willing pride, and yours is so.

*(Exit **KENT**.)*

PRINCESS
How does the king?
BOYET
Madam, sleeps still.
CORDELIA
O my dear father! Restoration hang
Thy medicine on my lips; and let this kiss
Repair those violent harms that my two sisters
Have in thy reverence made!

KING LEAR
                              Kind and dear princess!
PRINCESS
He wakes; speak to him.
CORDELIA
Madam, do you; 'tis fittest.
PRINCESS
How does my royal lord? How fares your majesty?
KING LEAR
Am I in France?
PRINCESS
                         In your own kingdom, sir.
KING LEAR
Do not abuse me.
You do me wrong to take me out o' the grave.
BOYET
He's scarce awake: let him alone awhile.
KING LEAR
Where have I been? Where am I? Fair daylight?
I will not swear these are my hands: let's see;
I feel this pin prick. Would I were assured
Of my condition!
CORDELIA
                    O, look upon me, sir,
And hold your hands in benediction o'er me:
No, sir, you must not kneel.
KING LEAR
                              Pray, do not mock me:
I am a very foolish fond old man;
And, to deal plainly,
I fear I am not in my perfect mind.
For, as I am a man, I think this lady
To be my child Cordelia.
CORDELIA
                         And so I am, I am.
KING LEAR
Be your tears wet? yes, faith. I pray, weep not:

If you have poison for me, I will drink it.
I know you do not love me; for your sisters
Have, as I do remember, done me wrong:
You have some cause, they have not.
CORDELIA
                                        No cause, no cause.
BOYET
Be comforted, good madam: the great rage,
You see, is kill'd in him: and yet it is danger
To make him even o'er the time he has lost.
Desire him to go in; trouble him no more
Till further settling.
PRINCESS
Will't please your highness walk?
KING LEAR
                                      You must bear with me:
Pray you now, forget and forgive: I am old and foolish.

(Exeunt.)

SCENE 3 - The French camp. Outside the princess' tent.

(Enter **EDGAR**, **JAQUENETTA** *and* **COSTARD**.*)*

EDGAR
>Here, mistress, take the shadow of this tree
>For your good host; pray that the right may thrive:
>If ever I return to you again, I'll bring you comfort.

JAQUENETTA
>Grace go with you, sir!

COSTARD
>I never knew man hold vile stuff so dear.
>Look, here's thy love: my foot and her face see.

EDGAR
>A bitter fool!

COSTARD
>Dost thou know the difference, my boy, between a bitter fool and a sweet fool?

EDGAR
>No, lad; teach me.

COSTARD
>A woman, master.

EDGAR
>*[To* **JAQUENETTA***]* One word in private with you, ere I die.

JAQUENETTA
>Bleat softly then; the butcher hears you cry.

EDGAR
>My point and period will be throughly wrought,
>Or well or ill, as this day's battle's fought.

(They converse apart. Drumming afar off. Enter the **PRINCESS**.*)*

PRINCESS
>Far off, methinks, I hear the beaten drum.

*(***JAQUENETTA** *leaps up.)*

JAQUENETTA
>You are deceived; 'tis not so.

EDGAR

Why is this reason'd?

JAQUENETTA

He's coming, madam; I hear him.
Near and on speedy foot.

SOLDIER

[Within] How now! What's the matter?

JAQUENETTA

Arms, arms, sword, fire! Corruption in the place!

PRINCESS

What's the matter there?

JAQUENETTA

Prepare, madam, prepare! you'll be surprised.

(Enter Soldiers of Navarre, in a skirmish. They surround and capture the **PRINCESS**, **EDGAR**, **JAQUENETTA** *and* **COSTARD**. **EDMUND** *enters, in conquest, to survey the prisoners.)*

EDMUND

[To **JAQUENETTA***]* A proclaim'd prize! Most happy!
That eyeless head of thine was first framed flesh
To raise my fortunes. *[To* **COSTARD***]* Thou fool, unhappy traitor,
Briefly thyself remember: the sword is out
That must destroy thee.
[To **PRINCESS***]* And here's another, whose warp'd looks proclaim
What store her heart is made on. Have I caught thee?

PRINCESS

Let go, slave, or thou diest!

(The **PRINCESS** *strikes him and tries to escape.)*

EDMUND

                    Stop her there!
Weapons! arms!

(Another skirmish. The **PRINCESS** *is recaptured. Enter a Captain with* **KING LEAR** *and* **CORDELIA***.)*

CAPTAIN

The king is here, he and his daughter ta'en.

EDMUND

Some officers take them away: good guard,
Until their greater pleasures first be known
That are to censure them.

CORDELIA

                              We are not the first
Who, with best meaning, have incurr'd the worst.
Shall we not see these daughters and these sisters?

KING LEAR

No, no, no, no! Come, let's away to prison:
We two alone will sing like birds i' the cage.

EDMUND

Take them away.

(Exeunt **KING LEAR** *and* **CORDELIA**, *guarded.)*

           [Aside] I hold their lives in mercy,
But there are sisters a-coming will speak their mind in
some other sort.
As for the mercy
Which may intend to Lear and to Cordelia:
The battle done, and they within my power,
Shall never see a pardon.
Come hither, Costard, hark. I pray you, go
Along with me.

COSTARD

                O, cry your mercy, sir.

EDMUND

Take thou this note; go follow them to prison:
One step I have advanced thee; if thou dost
As this instructs thee, thou dost make thy way
To noble fortunes.

(Gives him a shilling and a paper.)

All friends shall taste
The wages of their virtue, and all foes
The cup of their deservings.

COSTARD

Gardon, O sweet gardon! better than remuneration,
a'leven-pence farthing better: most sweet gardon!

EDMUND
> Thy great employment
> Will not bear question; either say thou'lt do 't,
> Or thrive by other means.

COSTARD
>   I'll do 't, my lord.
> I cannot draw a cart, nor eat dried oats;
> If it be man's work, I'll do 't.

EDMUND
> About it; and write happy when thou hast done.
>
> *(Exit* **COSTARD**. *A flourish of trumpets within.)*
>
> Here comes Hecate in arms.
>
> *(Enter* **GONERIL**, **REGAN**, *and Soldiers.)*

GONERIL
> Sir, you have shown to-day your valiant strain,
> And fortune led you well: you have the captives
> That were the opposites of this day's strife:
> We do require them of you, so to use them
> As we shall find their merits and our safety
> May equally determine.

EDMUND
>   Thus I thought it fit
> To send the old and miserable king
> To some retention and appointed guard.
> With him I sent the princess;
> To-morrow, or at further space, to appear
> Where you shall hold your session.
> The question of Cordelia and her father
> Requires a fitter place.

GONERIL
>   Sir, by your patience,
> I hold you but a subject of this war,
> Not as a brother.

REGAN
>   That's as we list to grace him.
> Methinks our pleasure might have been demanded,
> Ere you had spoke so far. He led our powers;

Bore the commission of my place and person;
The which immediacy may well stand up,
And call itself your brother.
GONERIL
                                                Not so hot:
In his own grace he doth exalt himself,
More than in your addition.
REGAN
                                                In my rights,
By me invested, he compeers the best.
GONERIL
That were the most, if he should husband you.
REGAN
Jesters do oft prove prophets.
GONERIL
                                            Holla, holla!
That eye that told you so look'd but a-squint.
REGAN
Lady, I am not well; else I should answer
From a full-flowing stomach. General,
Take thou my soldiers, prisoners, patrimony;
Dispose of them, of me; the walls are thine:
Witness the world, that I create thee here
My lord and master.
GONERIL
                              Mean you to enjoy him?
REGAN
The let-alone lies not in your good will.
GONERIL
Nor in thine own.
REGAN
                            Hot-blooded sister, yes.
[To **EDMUND***]* Let the drum strike, and prove my title thine.

(Drumming off, nearer than before.)

GONERIL
What drum is that?

EDMUND
>My herald is return'd.
>
>*(Enter* **KENT***, disguised as Herald, with drum before.)*
>
>Save thee, Curan.

KENT
>And you, sir.

REGAN
>I am much deceived but I remember the style.

GONERIL
>How now, what art thou?
>
>*(***KENT*** throws off his disguise.)*

EDMUND
>Break off, break off!

KENT
>How do you, sir? Stand you not so amazed:
>'Tis noble Kent, your friend.

EDMUND
>   Arm, wenches, arm!
>
>*(Enter Soldiers of the French power.)*
>
>Ladies, withdraw: the traitors are at hand.

GONERIL
>Whip to our tents, as roes run o'er land.
>
>*(Another skirmish.* **KENT** *frees the* **PRINCESS**. **GONERIL** *and* **REGAN** *are surrounded and* **EDMUND** *captured.)*

PRINCESS
>Now, you she foxes!
>Stay yet; hear reason. Edmund, I arrest thee
>On capital treason; and, in thine attaint,
>These gilded serpents.
>Come hither, herald,—Let the trumpet sound,
>And read out this.

KENT
>Sound, trumpet!
>
>*(A trumpet sounds.)*

[Reads] 'If any man of quality or degree within the lists of the army will maintain upon Edmund, supposed Earl of Gloucester, that he is a manifold traitor, let him appear at the sound of the trumpet: he is bold in his defence.'

REGAN

Thou art arm'd, Gloucester: let the trumpet sound.

PRINCESS

If none appear to prove upon thy head
Thy heinous, manifest, and many treasons,
There is my pledge;

(Throwing down a glove.)

      I'll prove it on thy heart,
Ere I taste bread, thou art in nothing less
Than I have here proclaim'd thee.

REGAN

          Sick, O, sick!

GONERIL

[Aside] If not, I'll ne'er trust medicine.

EDMUND

There's my exchange:

(Throwing down a glove.)

       what in the world he is
That names me traitor, villain-like he lies:
On him, on you, who not? I will maintain
My truth and honour firmly.

EDGAR

      [Advancing] Draw thy sword,
That, if my speech offend a noble heart,
Thy arm may do thee justice: here is mine.
This sword, this arm, and my best spirits, are bent
To prove upon thy heart, whereto I speak:
Thou art a traitor;
False to thy gods, thy brother, and thy father;
Conspirant 'gainst the high-illustrious king;
And, from the extremest upward of thy head

To the descent and dust below thy foot,
A most toad-spotted traitor.

EDMUND

Why dost thou use me thus? I know thee not.

EDGAR

What a brazen-faced varlet art thou, to deny thou knowest me!

REGAN

[To **EDMUND***]* What was the offence you gave him?

EDMUND

I never gave him any.

EDGAR

For your claim, fair Regan,
I bar it in thine interest as my wife:
'Tis she is sub-contracted to this lord,
And I, her husband, contradict the banns.

REGAN

You lie, you are not he.

GONERIL

      An interlude!

REGAN

What mean you, sirrah? by my life, my troth,
I never swore this fellow such an oath.

EDMUND

By rule of knighthood, I disdain and spurn:
Back do I toss these treasons to thy head;
This sword of mine shall give them instant way,
Where they shall rest for ever. Trumpets, speak!

(Alarums. They fight. **EDMUND** *falls.)*

REGAN

Save him, save him!

GONERIL

     This is practise, Gloucester:
By the law of arms thou wast not bound to answer
An unknown opposite; thou art not vanquish'd,
But cozen'd and beguiled.

REGAN

My sickness grows upon me.

PRINCESS

She is not well; convey her to my tent.

(Exit **REGAN**, *led by* **JAQUENETTA**.*)*

EDMUND

What you have charged me with, that have I done;
And more, much more; the time will bring it out:
'Tis past, and so am I. But what art thou
That hast this fortune on me? If thou'rt noble,
I do forgive thee.

EDGAR

                Let's exchange charity.
My name is Edgar, and thy father's son.
The dark and vicious place where thee he got
Cost him his life.

GONERIL

Methought thy very gait did prophesy
A royal nobleness: I must embrace thee:
Let sorrow split my heart, if ever I
Did hate thee or thy father!

EDGAR

Shut your mouth, dame,
Or with this paper shall I stop it: Hold, sir:
Thou worse than any name, read thine own evil:
No tearing, lady: I perceive you know it.

GONERIL

Say, if I do, the laws are mine, not thine:
Who can arraign me for't.

PRINCESS

                            Most monstrous! oh!
Know'st thou this paper?

GONERIL

Ask me not what I know.

(Exit.)

PRINCESS

Go after her: she's desperate; govern her.

EDGAR

I am no less in blood than thou art, Edmund;
If more, the more thou hast wrong'd me.

EDMUND

Thou hast spoken right, 'tis true;
The wheel is come full circle: I am here.
For mine own part, I breathe free breath. I have seen the day of wrong through the little hole of discretion, and I will right myself like a soldier.

*(Enter **JAQUENETTA**, with a bloody knife.)*

JAQUENETTA

Help, help, O, help!

EDGAR

                        What kind of help?

PRINCESS

                                    Speak, lass.

EDGAR

What means that bloody knife?

JAQUENETTA

                               'Tis hot, it smokes;
It came even from the heart of—O, she's dead!

EDGAR

Who dead? speak, lass.

JAQUENETTA

My lady, sir, my lady: and her sister
By her is poisoned; she hath confess'd it.

EDMUND

I was contracted to them both: all three
Now marry in an instant.

PRINCESS

Produce their bodies, be they alive or dead:
This judgment of the heavens, that makes us tremble,
Touches us not with pity.

*(The bodies of **GONERIL** and **REGAN** are brought in.)*

EDMUND

Yet Edmund was beloved:
The one the other poison'd for my sake,
And after slew herself.

KENT

[To a Soldier] Come hither, friend: where is the king my master?
Is he not here?

PRINCESS

                Great thing of us forgot!
Speak, Edmund, where's the king? and where's Cordelia?

EDMUND

I pant for life: some good I mean to do,
Despite of mine own nature. Quickly send,
Be brief in it, to the castle; for my writ
Is on the life of Lear and on Cordelia:
Nay, send in time.

KENT

Run, run, O, run!

PRINCESS

Haste thee, for thy life.

    (Exit **KENT**.*)*

EDMUND

He hath commission in a note from me
To hang Cordelia in the prison, and
To lay the blame upon her own despair,
That she fordid herself.

PRINCESS

The gods defend her! Bear him hence awhile.

    (**EDMUND** *is borne off. Re-enter* **KING LEAR**, *with* **CORDELIA** *limp in his arms;* **KENT**, *and others following.*)

KING LEAR

Howl, howl, howl, howl! O, you are men of stones:
Had I your tongues and eyes, I'd use them so
That heaven's vault should crack. She's gone for ever!

I know when one is dead, and when one lives;
She's dead as earth. Lend me a looking-glass;
If that her breath will mist or stain the stone,
Why, then she lives.
KENT
Is this the promised end?

EDGAR

Or image of that horror?

PRINCESS
Fall, and cease!

KING LEAR

A plague upon you, murderers, traitors all!
I might have saved her; now she's gone for ever!
Cordelia, Cordelia! stay a little. Ha!
What is't thou say'st? Her voice was ever soft,
Gentle, and low, an excellent thing in woman.
I kill'd the knave that was a-hanging thee.

KENT

'Tis true, my lords, he did.

KING LEAR
Did I not, fellow?

I have seen the day, with my good biting falchion
I would have made them skip: I am old now,
And these same crosses spoil me.

PRINCESS

Your eldest daughters have fordone them selves,
And desperately are dead.

KING LEAR
Ay, so I think.

And my poor fool is hang'd! No, no, no life!
Why should a dog, a horse, a rat, have life,
And thou no breath at all? Thou'lt come no more,
Never, never, never, never, never!

KENT

O, see, see!

KING LEAR

This feather stirs; she lives! if it be so,

It is a chance which does redeem all sorrows
That ever I have felt.
Pray you, undo this button: thank you, sir.
Do you see this? Look on her, look, her lips,
Look there, look there!

   (Dies.)

EDGAR

                     He faints! My lord, my lord!

PRINCESS

Break, heart; I prithee, break!

EDGAR

                          Look up, my lord.

PRINCESS

Vex not his ghost: O, let him pass! he hates him much
That would upon the rack of this tough world
Stretch him out longer.

EDGAR

                       He is gone, indeed.

PRINCESS

The wonder is, he hath endured so long:
He but usurp'd his life.

   (Enter **BOYET**.*)*

BOYET

Edmund is dead, my lords.

PRINCESS

That's but a trifle here.

   (**CORDELIA** *wakes.*)

KENT

God save you, madam!

CORDELIA

                       Welcome, noble Kent;
But that thou interrupt'st our merriment.

PRINCESS

She knows not what she says.

CORDELIA
> Will you not dance? How come you thus estranged?

KENT
> I am sorry, madam; for the news I bring
> Is heavy in my tongue. The king your father—

CORDELIA
> Dead, for my life!

KENT
>   Even so; my tale is told.

PRINCESS
> Worthies, away! the scene begins to cloud.

KENT
> Yet, since love's argument was first on foot,
> Let not the cloud of sorrow justle it
> From what it purposed; since, to wail friends lost
> Is not by much so wholesome-profitable
> As to rejoice at friends but newly found.

CORDELIA
> I understand you not: my griefs are double.

KENT
> Honest plain words best pierce the ear of grief;
> And by these badges understand thy Kent.
> For your fair sakes have we neglected time,
> Play'd foul play with our oaths: your beauty, ladies,
> Hath much deform'd us, fashioning our humours
> Even to the opposèd end of our intents:
> Our love being yours, the error that love makes
> Is likewise yours: we to ourselves prove false,
> By being once false for ever to be true
> To those that make us both,—fair ladies, you.

CORDELIA
> No, no, my lord, your grace is perjured much:
> Your oath I will not trust; but go with speed
> To some forlorn and naked hermitage;
> There stay until the twelve celestial signs
> Have brought about the annual reckoning.
> If this austere insociable life

Change not your offer made in heat of blood;
Then, at the expiration of the year,
I will be thine; and till that instant shut
My woeful self up in a mourning house
For the remembrance of my father's death.
If this thou do deny, let our hands part,
Neither entitled in the other's heart.

KENT

If this, or more than this, I would deny,
The sudden hand of death close up mine eye!

EDGAR

I am a votary; I have vowed to Jaquenetta to hold the plough for her sweet love a year.
I'll stay with patience; but the time is long.

JAQUENETTA

The liker you; few taller are so young.

PRINCESS

Bear them from hence. Our present business
Is general woe. *[To* **KENT** *and* **EDGAR***]* Friends of my soul, you twain
Rule in this realm, and the gored state sustain.
The weight of this sad time we must obey;
Speak what we feel, not what we ought to say.
The oldest hath borne most: we that are young
Shall never see so much, nor live so long.
My sweet Cordelia, so I take my leave.

CORDELIA

No, madam; we will bring you on your way.

KENT

Our wooing doth not end like an old play;
Jack hath not Jill: these ladies' courtesy
Might well have made our sport a comedy.

EDGAR

Come, sir, it wants a twelvemonth and a day,
And then 'twill end.

KENT

                That's too long for a play.

PRINCESS
> The words of love are harsh after the songs of war. You that way: we this way.
>
> *(Exeunt severally.)*

End of Act V

END OF PLAY

Also by
Jeff Goode

The Eight: Reindeer Monologues

Ham/thello: The Moor of Denmark

The Messy Adventures of Dick Piston, Hotel Detective

Princess Gray and the Black & White Knights

Romeo and Julius [Caesar]

Rumpelstiltskin

Seven Santas

The Ubu Plays

Your Swash Is Unbuckled

Please consult the
Baker's Plays Catalogue
for complete details or find us online at
www.bakersplays.com

After The Rain King
By Steph DeFerie

Full Length / 4m, 4w, 6 m or f or as many as 22 can be cast / Single set with additions. Glory may be just a little kid but she's in big trouble - when she accidentally opens an old, locked book she finds in an old trunk, a mysterious stranger jumps out! "I am the Rain King, The Lord Of Tears, The Master Of Sorrows, The Commander of the Darkness in your soul! I suck the happiness from your thought and leave only fear and desolation. Destruction is my bread and butter, loss is my meat and drink!" And Glory is the one responsible for releasing him from his prison and setting him free in the world again! Before she can stop him, he kidnaps Pete and disappears back into the book. To rescue Pete, Glory and her friends must follow and soon find themselves jumping from story to story - battling pirates in "Treasure Island", helping young Arthur pull the sword from the stone in "Le Morte D'arthur" facing down bank robbers in "Prairie Rustlers" and even becoming bugs! Can they save Pete, not to mention the rest of the world, from this dangerous monster or will he cast his evil spell over us all. A funny chilling and imaginative play with an exciting climax.

Please visit our website
bakersplays.com
for complete descriptions and licensing information

www.ingramcontent.com/pod-product-compliance
Lightning Source LLC
Chambersburg PA
CBHW051449290426
44109CB00016B/1684